An Historical Account Of The Rise And Progress Of The Bengal Native Infantry: From Its First Formation In 1757, To 1796 When The Present Regulations Took Place, Together With A Detail Of The Services On Which The Several Battalions Have Been Employed

John Williams (Captain.)

Subadar.

AN

HISTORICAL ACCOUNT

OF THE

RISE AND PROGRESS

OF THE

BENGAL NATIVE INFANTRY,

FROM ITS FIRST FORMATION

IN 1757, TO 1796,

WHEN THE PRESENT REGULATIONS TOOK PLACE.

TOGETHER WITH A

DETAIL OF THE SERVICES

ON WHICH THE SEVERAL BATTALIONS HAVE BEEN EMPLOYED

DURING THAT PERIOD.

———————

BY THE LATE

CAPTAIN WILLIAMS,

OF THE INVALID ESTABLISHMENT OF THE BENGAL ARMY.

———————

LONDON:

JOHN MURRAY, ALBEMARLE STREET.

1817.

London: Printed by C. Roworth,
Bell-yard, Temple-bar.

THE FOLLOWING

HISTORICAL ACCOUNT

OF THE RISE AND PROGRESS OF

THE BENGAL NATIVE INFANTRY,

Which (down to the year 1796) employed the leisure hours
of the late

CAPTAIN JOHN WILLIAMS,

AN OLD AND ZEALOUS SOLDIER

OF THE

HONOURABLE EAST INDIA COMPANY'S SERVICE,

ON THE BENGAL ESTABLISHMENT;

And continued to the present period,

BY A BROTHER OFFICER

Of the same Service;

IS INSCRIBED

TO THE

RIGHT HONOURABLE THE BOARD OF CONTROUL,

AND TO THE

HONOURABLE THE COURT OF DIRECTORS

OF THE

EAST INDIA COMPANY,

IN TESTIMONY OF RESPECT

FOR THOSE HIGH AUTHORITIES,

PRESIDING OVER THE AFFAIRS OF THE

BRITISH EMPIRE

IN ASIA.

London, December, 1816.

THE Bengal Native Infantry have been long noticed for their good conduct and gallantry in the field; and as some of the battalions have, upon all occasions, distinguished themselves in a particular manner, many old officers have expressed their concern that no minute account had been published of them, especially those in the early part of the service. The writer of this has undertaken the task at the request of some very respectable officers, although he is conscious of his inability to do justice to the subject. He hopes and trusts, however, that his endeavours may be favourably received by those for whose amusement they are intended, and allowance made for any errors which may occur in the following sheets, when he informs

B

them that he has scarcely a document but his own memory to guide him. He owns that the task is in some measure pleasing to him, as it recals to his mind many of the early scenes of his youth, which is gratifying to every man advanced in years, but particularly so to an old soldier, who has been near half a century in the profession.

It is his intention to give the best account he can of the several battalions, from the time of their being raised until the year 1796, when the present establishment took place.

AN

HISTORICAL ACCOUNT,

&c. &c. &c.

Prior to the year 1757, the military A.D.1756. establishment of Bengal consisted of only one company of Artillery and four or five companies of European Infantry, with a few hundred Natives, armed after the manner of the country, for the protection of the several factories. After Calcutta was taken by the Nabob Surajah Dowlah, the Council of Madras ordered Lord Clive and Major Kilpàtrick round to Bengal, with such a detachment of their troops as could be spared, so as not to endanger the safety of their own settlement. As several companies of Sepoys accompanied that detachment, these men laid the foundation of the Bengal Native Infantry.

1757.   In January, 1757, on the retaking of Calcutta and re-establishment of the Government, a battalion of Sepoys was ordered to be raised and officered from the Madras detachment.   That battalion is still in being, and will be treated of in its present rank.   In the course of that year, some other battalions were formed, and officered in like manner.*

The establishment of a battalion of Native Infantry was then one captain, one lieutenant and one ensign, who acted as field officers; and the subalterns had two rupees per day extra for their trouble in disciplining their men, in which they

---

* In the month of June this year (1757) the battle of Plassey was fought, in which about 2,000 Sepoys were engaged.   The present 2d battalion 12th regiment was in that battle.

were assisted by a serjeant-major and a
few serjeants. There was a Native commandant, who took post in front with the
captain, and a Native adjutant, who remained in the rear with the subalterns.
The battalion consisted of ten companies,
two of which were grenadiers, as at present. Each company had a subadar, three
jemadars, five hawuldars, (one of which
was a colour man,) four naicks, two tomtoms,* one trumpeter, and seventy Sepoys. Each company had a stand of colours attached to it, of the same colour as
the facings of the men; in the center of
which was the subiadar's device or badge,
such as a sabre, a dagger, a crescent, &c.
and the Grenadiers, by way of distinction,
had the British Union in the upper corner.

When two or more battalions did duty 1764.
together, they took post according to the

* A small Indian drum,

B 3

date of their captain's commission; but as that mode created some confusion, in frequently changing corps from one part of the line to another, the Governor and Council, in April, 1764, ordered the bat-talions to be numbered according to the then rank of their captains, which was as follows, being eighteen in number, viz.—

1. Captain Giles Stibbert.
2. Captain M'Lean.
3. Captain Hugh Grant.
4. Captain Campbell.
5.
6. Captain Trevanion.
7. Captain Brown.
8. Captain William Smith.
9. Captain P. Galliez.
10. Captain Ironside.
11. Captain James Morgan.
12. Captain John White.
13. Captain Swinton.

14. Captain Hampton.
15. Captain Stables.
16. Captain Scotland.
17. Captain Goddard.
18. Captain Dow.

Shortly after, another battalion was raised by the Town Major in Calcutta, and numbered the Nineteenth.

On the arrival of Lord Clive in 1765, he found the Bengal army to consist of twenty-four companies of European infantry, four companies of artillery, a troop of hussars, and about twelve hundred irregular cavalry, with the Sepoys as above.

As soon as peace was concluded with Sujah Dowlah, the hussars were dismounted and incorporated with the infantry, and the irregular cavalry dismissed, except three hundred. His Lordship ordered two more battalions to be raised, and then divided the whole into three divisions or

1765.

brigades, except one company of artillery which was set apart for the duty of Fort William. Each brigade consisted of a Rossalah or troop of cavalry, one company of artillery, one regiment of European infantry of nine companies, and seven battalions of Sepoys, as follows:—

1st Brigade.	2d Brigade.	3d Brigade.
2d	1st	6th
3d	7th	9th
4th	8th	11th
5th	15th	12th
10th	16th	14th
13th	18th	19th
17th	20th to be raised	21st to be raised.

1766. In 1766, his Lordship, having obtained from the Emperor Shah Allum, the Dewanee, or management of the revenues, of the Bengal provinces, ordered a battalion from each brigade to be turned over to the Revenue Department; but they were to retain their rank in the line, and continued on the strength of their brigades. At the same time he ordered six new battalions to be formed for the same duty, which were denominated Purgunnah or Provincial Battalions. Those corps, although numbered in the line, were solely dependant on the Revenue Board.

In 1773, in consequence of some misconduct of the Purgunnah battalions, in the northern parts of Bengal, against the Senasses,* the three old battalions were returned to their brigades, and the new ones broke, except the 24th, which was then on particular duty at Ramgur, under the command of Captain Camac.

At the same time an alteration took place in the rest of the Native establishment. The extra pay to Sepoy subalterns was discontinued, and an allowance of one rupee per day was added to the pay of all the subalterns in the service. The number of subalterns in each battalion was in-

* Itinerant tribes of religious fanatics and marauders.

creased to three lieutenants and three ensigns. The colours were taken from the
several companies, and only two stand allowed to the battalion, as in the European
regiment, which were in future to be carried by jemadars. All the tomtoms and
trumpeters were dismissed, and drums and
fifes substituted.

In 1775, General Clavering, having then
the command of the army, thought it
would appear better on the official returns,
if the battalions were regularly numbered
in their several brigades; he therefore gave
the seven first numbers to the first brigade,
the next seven to the second brigade, and
the seven last numbers to the third brigade. This changed the number of every
battalion in the service except the twenty-
first. The 7th battalion, then at Chitta-
gong, was made independent, and the
24th battalion at Ramgur was brought

into the line in its stead, and numbered the Fourteenth.

In 1778, war breaking out with the Maharattas, and afterwards with the French, six battalions from the first brigade were ordered across the country to the west of India, and some new battalions were formed to replace them; and several battalions, which had been disciplined by British officers for the service of the Vizier, were taken into the Company's service.

In the latter end of the year 1780, in consequence of the defeat of Colonel Ballie's detachment, and the irruption of Hyder Ally into the Carnatic, the Government of Bengal deemed it requisite to augment their army, that they might be enabled to send succours to the coast: accordingly a new establishment of the Native infantry took place. Every battalion in the service, except the six at

Bombay, was increased to a thousand
men, and formed into a regiment, consisting of two battalions—each battalion of
five companies. A major commanded the
regiment, and a captain each battalion,
with a lieutenant to each company under
him, but no ensigns. This had effect from
the 1st of January, 1781, immediately
after which five regiments were ordered to
Madras under Colonel Pearse.*

1785—6. In the beginning of 1786 a new establishment was formed. The two battalions
of each regiment were doubled up into
a single battalion of ten companies, and
the number of battalions reduced to thirty; ten to each brigade; and all the In-
dependant Corps were reduced.

This arrangement had scarcely taken
effect, when orders for a revised establishment arrived from Europe. The army

* Viz. the 12th, 13th, 24th, 25th, and 26th regiments.

was accordingly formed into six brigades, each consisting of a battalion of Europeans, and six battalions of Sepoys, of eight companies each; which increased the number of battalions to thirty-six. In 1791 the war with Tippoo Sultan breaking out, six battalions were ordered to the coast;* and the whole of the Native corps were augmented to ten companies each, which system continued in force until the present establishment was fixed in 1796.

The battalions which were in the service in the year 1764, have already been mentioned, as well as those which were afterwards formed to complete the brigades; but as four of those battalions are not now in being, the writer trusts that an account of them will not be unacceptable. They will be spoken of as they stood, when they were numbered, the 7th, 15th, 19th, and 24th.

* Viz. the 3d, 7th, 13th, 14th, 26th, and 28th battalions.

The 7th battalion was raised at Chitta-gong in 1758, and remained constantly in that province, and of course had little opportunity of distinguishing itself. In 1764 it was commanded by Captain Brown, and he being the seventh upon the list it became that number. In 1765 it was posted to the 2d brigade; and when General Clavering's arrangement took place, in 1775, it became an independent corps, and as such was reduced in 1786.

The 15th battalion was an old and dis-tinguished corps. It was raised in Cal-cutta, the latter end of the year 1757, by a Captain Mathews, whose name it went by as long as it existed—a name which both officers and men were proud to boast of.

In 1758 it accompanied Colonel Ford to Masulapatam, where its conduct in the action with the French, before that for-tress, was highly spoken of. In 1759 it

returned to Bengal, and early the following year was detached, with the same
officer, to attack the Dutch troops which
were intended to be smuggled into Bengal, as was supposed, by the connivance
of the Nabob Meer Jaffier. Colonel Ford
came up with them near Ghyretty, and
gave them a total defeat, taking the
greatest part of them prisoners. The
Mathews did its duty fully upon that occasion, as it did during the remainder of the
year under Colonel Caillaud. Early in
1761 it was one of the battalions with
Major Carnac, when he defeated and took
prisoner the Shah Zadah, afterwards Emperor. It remained at Patna until 1762,
when the greatest part of the army returned to Calcutta, where it remained until the war broke out with Cossim Ally, in
June, 1763, when it was again early in the
field under Majors Adams and Carnac,

and behaved with great bravery during
the whole of that arduous campaign,
which was carried on in the height of the
rains; but particularly at the battle of
Gheria, which was fought on the 2d of
August, near Sooty. The enemy's cavalry
having broke through the Company's
European troops, whilst they were forming, this battalion, and some others, nobly
supported the 84th regiment, and gained a
complete victory. The European battalion, although thrown into some confusion
by the sudden attack of the cavalry, soon
recovered their order, and had ample satisfaction of the enemy.

Major Adams pursued Cossim Ally's
troops to Uddah Nullah, where they made
a stand; and, it being a strong position,
would have given the army a great deal of
trouble, had not the Major ordered a detachment of Europeans and Sepoys to

take a circular march by the foot of the hills, during the night, so that at day-break the next morning, they were com-pletely surprized, and a dreadful slaughter, at the point of the bayonet, was the con-sequence, after which they scarcely ever faced him, not even at the Pass of Ter-riagully, which, at that time, might have been defended by one hundred men against a thousand.

The army, on getting clear of the hills, pushed on to Monghyr, which made but a feeble resistance ; and having thrown a small garrison into the place, the Major continued his march towards Patna; but Cossim Ally having broken down an arch of the bridge over the Daccra Nulla, he was detained one day in laying planks for the army to cross. The broken arch remains in the same state at this day.. On the ar-rival of the army at Patna, that city was immediately invested. It held out for some days, and was then taken by storm, in which Captain Irving of the 84th regiment was killed, and Lieutenant Galliez, with one or two other officers, whose names the writer cannot now recollect, were wounded, and several non-commissioned officers and privates killed and wounded. From thence the Major pursued the enemy, (who were flying towards Sujah Dowlah's country, by the road of Dowdnagur and Sassaram,) and in about ten days reached the Carumnassa, a small river which then separated the dominions of the Vizier from those of the Company. Here he halted about a week, and then marched back to Sant, a small village on the banks of the Durgotty, a nulla which runs parallel with the Carumnassa, and about four miles from it. Major Adams left the army at Sant, and proceeded to Calcutta, where he died in January, 1764.

On his departure the command devolved on Major Jennings of the Artillery, who, to his great concern, soon discovered a spirit of disaffection and insubordination amongst the troops. It seems some promises were made them on taking the field, by the Nabob Meer Jaffier, which were not fulfilled; and now that Major Adams had left them, under whom they had fought, and through whom the promise had been made, they despaired of ever being recompensed for their bravery. This occasioned the ill humour which was then so visible in the army. On a certain day the whole line got under arms without orders, threatening to march into Sujah Dowlah's country, and throw themselves on his protection if their donation was not instantly paid; and the Europeans actually began their march towards the Carumnassa. However, by the persuasion of the officers and serjeants, all the British, and some few of the German soldiers, were brought back; and Serjeant Delamar, formerly of the 84th regiment, who, being of French parents, although born in London, spoke the language as fluently as he did English, was sent after them to try and prevail on them to return, with a promise of promotion in case he succeeded. He accordingly mounted his tattoo,* and overtook them about a mile from the Carumnassa; but instead of using his endeavours to bring them to a sense of their duty, he placed himself at the head of them, observing, " that now was the time to make their fortunes, and if they would follow him he would lead them to riches and honour." They gave him three cheers, and then pushed on to the Carumnassa. Here many more of the Germans,

* Small horse.

seeing that the French were carrying things farther than they intended, quitted them, and returned to Sant during the night. Next morning it was found that we had lost about two hundred men.*

* It may appear strange how so many of the French nation could get into the service of Bengal at that early period: the cause of it shall therefore be explained. In January, 1761, Pondicherry, the only fortress the French had then remaining in India, surrendered to Sir Eyre Coote. The garrison of that city was composed of the old French regiment of Lorraine, Lally's Irish regiment, and the French Company's regiment, called the Pondicherry—a great number of the men of these regiments enlisted in the Company's service. Those from Lally's were incorporated with the British troops; but the men of the Lorraine and Pondicherry were formed into two independent companies. All the others, being prisoners of war, were sent to Bengal, where, on the commencement of the troubles with Cossim Ally, a number of them engaged in the Company's service, and were placed under M. Claude Martine, their countryman, who had formerly served in the Lorraine regiment. M. Martine afterwards got a commission, and died a Major General in the Honourable Company's army.

The two companies left at Madras were, in the year 1762, embarked on board Admiral Cornish's fleet, and accompanied it to Manilla, where they were found very

The Sepoy battalions had put them selves in motion to follow the Europeans;

useful in making gabions, fascines, and pickets, for carrying on the approaches. The place was taken by storm on the 6th of October; after which the Admiral took possession of Cavitta, where finding excellent docks, and plenty of naval stores, with a great number of good Malay and Chinese carpenters, he thought it right to give his ships a thorough repair before he returned to the Indian seas: this took him up until the end of February, 1763. Having arranged matters with the Governor, (a Mr. Drake, of the Madras Civil Service,) and with Major Fell, who commanded the troops, he fixed on the 1st of March for quitting the harbour, having ordered the Falmouth, a fifty gun ship, with Sir William Draper's regiment, and all the Company's troops, to remain for the protection of Manilla and the Port of Cavitta. But the night before he was to sail it was fortunately discovered, that the two French companies had entered into a conspiracy to surprize the city, and give it up to the Spaniards as soon as the fleet had put to sea. On information being sent to the Admiral he ordered out all the boats of the fleet, and in the course of the day, the two French companies were taken on board. Early next morning he quitted Manilla bay; but, owing to calms and light winds, did not reach Madras until the 18th of May, where he found the Liverpool frigate, just arrived from England, with an account of the peace between all the powers at war, and an order for Admiral Cornish to return home with the fleet. The two French companies were immediately landed.

but from the influence of the European
officers, who were highly respected by

Here the fleet remained until the latter end of August,
when accounts were received from Bengal of the war with
Cossim Ally, and the capture of the detachment at Patna.
It was immediately determined by the Council of Madras
to send a reinforcement to Bengal, and the Admiral agreed
to furnish two line of battle ships, and as many frigates,
completed to their full complement of Marines, for that
service. The ships ordered for this duty were the York
and Medway of sixty guns each, with the Argo and Liverpool of twenty-eight; and the Argo, being the quickest
sailer, was dispatched with information to the Bengal
government: she sailed from Madras on the 1st of September, and arrived off the Old Fort on the 9th, when the
Marines were immediately landed. Towards the end of
the month the rest of the fleet arrived under the command
of Commodore Tinker, when the Marines joined those of
the Argo, and the whole were ordered to Ghyretty. Here
they found their number to be about two hundred, commanded by Captain Frederick Thomas Smith,* (afterwards
in the Company's service, and Town Major of Fort William,) and Captain Maurice Wemys;† but there being
only two Marine subalterns in the four ships, the Commo-

* He became a Major in 1768, and died at Patna in
1770, then commanding the Purgunnah battalion at that
station.

† Died lately a Major General of Marines.

c 4

them, and the promise of Major Jennings
that their grievances should be laid before

dore commissioned a few of the midshipmen. About the
middle of October they marched to Burdwan to watch the
motions of the Maharattas, who had threatened to enter
Bengal during the troubles, where Major Carnac, who had
been ordered from the Grand Army, arrived and took the
command of them. Here they found Captain M'Lean's
battalion of Sepoys, and the Major brought with him the
troop of Hussars. Early in November they were joined
by a detachment of near three hundred Europeans from
Madras, amongst whom were their Manilla acquaintance,
the two French companies. The Major then moved towards Ramgur, along the Maharatta frontier; but before
he had marched above six days, he learnt from Calcutta,
that the Maharattas had dropt the design of entering these
provinces; he therefore ordered all the Company's troops
to proceed, by what is now called the New Road,* and
join the army under Major Adams at Sant, where they arrived about the end of December, and where, the writer
has no doubt but the two French companies were the
principal instigators of the mutiny, although they had nothing to complain of.

Major Carnac went down to Calcutta, and the Marines
marched back to Burdwan, where they remained until the

* A military road made by order of Mr. Hastings, after
the insurrection at Benares in 1781, to facilitate the communication with the upper provinces.

Government; and having distributed amongst them all the money he had in camp, they were prevailed on to return to their duty.

As soon as information of this unexpected transaction had reached Calcutta, the Government became alarmed for the safety of the country. An express was instantly sent to Commodore Tinker, requesting that the Marines might be relanded and sent off to join the army. The Commodore immediately repaired to town, with the Marines of the Medway, where they joined those of the Argo, then lying off the Old Fort, the whole amounting to one hundred privates complete, commanded by Captain Wemys. The York and Liverpool had sailed for Madras, with Captain Smith's company on board, a few days before.

latter end of January, 1764, when they embarked on board their respective ships in order to return to England.

As soon as the Marines under Captain Wemys had received their camp equipage, they were immediately sent off to the army, with which they formed a junction on the 9th of May, after a most fatiguing march in the hottest season of the year.

When Major Carnac heard of the business at Sant, he immediately set off by post to take the command of the army, where, on his arrival, finding that the ill humour into which the troops had been thrown was not quite subsided, and understanding that Sujah Dowlah, and the Emperor Shah Allum, were preparing to invade Bengal with a powerful army, for the express purpose of restoring Cossim Ally to the Musnud, he thought it right to march across the country to Buxar, where he encamped for a few days, when hearing that Sujah Dowlah had actually crossed the Carumnassa, he marched to Patna, and entrenched the army under the walls of that city. This was the middle of April; and about the same time the orders of Government were received for fixing the rank of Sepoy battalions, when the Mathews, then commanded by Captain Stables, became the Fifteenth in number.

Sujah Dowlah came before Patna about the 24th or 25th of April, and immediately invested both the city and the army, placing his right under Shah Allum, at Meer Jaffier's gardens, close to the river; his left under Cossim Ally, at Bankypore; and with the center he took post near Lohanapore, his whole line united, and something better than a mile in front of the British intrenchment. Hearing that the Marines were fast advancing he detached a strong body of cavalry to cut them off; but, fearing that they might give his detachment the slip, and get into

Patna, he prepared to attack Major Carnac, before he could receive any reinforcement;—accordingly on the 3d of May, having put every thing in order, his whole line advanced to the attack; but the Bengal troops were prepared for the meeting, and gave him so warm a reception, that after a contest of some hours, finding he could make no impression, he retired within his own lines. All the troops behaved remarkably well upon this occasion, but none more so than the battalion which is now treating of.

The Marines, on the 9th of May, (as has been already mentioned,) arrived in Patna from the opposite side of the Ganges, and about sun-set the Major met them at the west gate of the city, and conducted them to their post in the line of intrenchment,*

---

* The manner of doing duty, in this intrenchment, was very correct and judicious. Every evening at sun-set one

where they were received by the hearty cheers of their countrymen, as well as by all the Native soldiers in camp.

Here they remained, looking at each other, until about noon on the 30th of May, when the enemy's troops were perceived to be in motion, bending their march towards their own left. The drums immediately beat to arms, and the Marines, with the grenadiers and four companies of grenadier Sepoys, under the

third of each corps formed a piquet, which immediately mounted the rampart, and sent out a triple row of double sentries—the farthest about one hundred and fifty yards from the ditch, and the two inner rows at fifty paces distance from each other. If the outward sentries perceived any thing which had a suspicious appearance, they were to fire their pieces and retire to the next row, and so on until the cause of alarm was discovered. At eight o'clock the remainder of the army mounted the rampart, and after that not a man was allowed to quit his rank, but to sleep on his arms until it was broad day, when the whole retired to their tents. The piquets relieved the sentries every hour, by one of the corporals; and one of the serjeants visited them every half hour between the reliefs.

command of Captain Wemys, were ordered out to harass their rear; but they found it so well protected, that they could make little impression. They exchanged a few shot, but it was thought without injury to either side. They were, however, much galled, as they passed the right of the line, by a few guns which were placed on a commanding spot of ground within the intrenchment.

The following day, on hearing that the combined army had continued its march towards Moneah, a detachment was formed for the purpose of clearing the Sircar Sarun district, which had been overrun by some of Sujah Dowlah's troops and irregulars, and to prevent their getting any succours from their Grand Army. This detachment consisted of the Marines, and the Company's Grenadiers, with the Battalions of Captains Trevanion, Galliez, and

Stables, and commanded by Major Champion.. Early the next morning, being the 1st of June, they marched down to the Old Factory, where they were joined by eight guns, six and three pounders. The European troops immediately embarked, with as many of the Native troops as the boats could carry, and landed a little above Hadjepore. As soon as the whole had crossed they moved to a good spot of ground and encamped. The following morning they commenced their march, and continued it every day, without seeing an enemy, until they reached Sewan, on the banks of the Gogra, which being the boundary of the Company's territories, they halted, and remained some days; when finding that the province was entirely clear of the enemy, and that the rains were daily expected to set in, they marched back, and on passing Manjee, the Marines and Captain Galliez's battalion were ordered to halt; but the rest of the detachment went on to Choprah, where they were to canton during the rains, except the grenadiers, who were directed to proceed to the head-quarters of the army, then fixed at Bankypore. The Marines moved into the Fort of Manjee, and the battalion took up its quarters in the town. A few days after their arrival, Captain Wemys being desirous of having a small Bunglo on one of the angles of the fort, the people were set to work upon it, and, on sinking the posts, discovered a deposit of small arms, five and twenty in number, of the years 1760—61, supposed to have belonged to the unfortunate Patna detachment, which shall be mentioned hereafter. Here the Marines remained until the beginning of August, when temporary barracks at Choprah being prepared for them, they marched into them; but the battalion was left at Manjee. About three weeks or a month after the Marines left them a serious mutiny broke out, and the battalion marched off. On information reaching Choprah, the Marines and Captain Trevanion's battalion, under the command of Captain Wemys, were sent after them; and after two days very fatiguing march, every step almost up to the knees in water, came up with them. The mutineers had got into a mango tope, or grove, on a high spot, surrounded with water, which was scarcely fordable. On seeing the detachment, they drew up at the edge of the grove, and seemed determined to dispute the point with them. However, we* moved down, and drew up facing them, and after a little

* The author of this narrative belonged at that period to the Marines.

conversation they agreed to surrender. Rafts were then constructed, when the mutineers were brought over and disarmed, and the whole conducted prisoners to Choprah, where a severe example was made, and the battalion ordered over to Patna. The particulars of this mutiny, and the consequences attending it, shall be noticed when the writer comes to speak of that battalion.

Early in the month of October, 1764, preparations were made for uniting the army, in order to march towards Sujah Dowlah, who had cantoned at Buxar, during the rains. On the 6th, in the morning, boats being ready, the whole of the detachment, with the guns, were embarked, under as heavy a storm of rain as can be imagined, which continued the whole of that and the two following days; but on the 9th it cleared up, and the evening of that day they reached the mouth of the Soane, where they disembarked, and encamped on the western bank of the river, on such dry spots as they could find, without separating the corps too much.

At two o'clock the next morning they took up their line of march, and moved along the bank of the Soane, towards the ferry, opposite to Moneah, until day-break, when Hircarahs came in and reported, that Major Munro, with the Grand Army, were at Moneah, and preparing to cross the river; that a large body of the enemy were drawn up to oppose his landing; and that we were within a short mile of them. On this the detachment immediately halted, and formed in order of battle; the Marines in the center; Captain Trevanion's on the right; and the Mathews on the left, with the guns in the intervals. By this time, the haze of the morning having cleared away, they had a distinct view of the enemy, who, on perceiving them, changed their front towards the detachment. Every thing being now ready, Major Champion ordered three guns to be fired quick, which was the signal agreed on with Major Munro. It was immediately answered from the other side of the river, and in a few minutes after the detachment heard the Grenadier's March, which at that time was music of the most pleasing kind to them. They then pushed on to attack the enemy, who, after exchanging a few shot with them, retired towards Arrah. They continued their march to the Ferry, where they had, in a short time, the satisfaction of seeing their old companions the Grenadiers, with all the other European corps, and two battalions of Sepoys, being the first embarkation, safely landed. The rest of the troops, with

the guns and baggage, came over in the
course of the day, when the whole encamped, about half a mile from the Ferry,
on the road leading to Arrah.

When the returns of the several corps
were collected, it was found that the
army consisted of eight complete battalions of Sepoys, with the two companies of
Grenadiers, which had accompanied the
Marines from Monghyr, and about eleven
or twelve hundred irregular cavalry, with
eight hundred and fifty-seven Europeans,
making in the whole about eight thousand
men, with two and twenty field pieces.
Major Munro,* who had just arrived from
Bombay, commanded in chief, with Majors
Champion, Stibbert, and Pemble to assist
him, and Major Jennings commanding the
Artillery. Here they halted the two following days, during which time the order

* The late General Sir Hector Munro, K. B.

of battle was arranged, which it was determined should be an oblong square, as a great part of the enemy's force was cavalry. There being parties of four of his Majesty's corps in the field, viz. 84th, 89th, and 90th regiments, with the Marines, making in the whole something less than two hundred men, they were formed into a battalion under Captain Wemys of the Marines.

Every thing being prepared for marching against the enemy, the army left their ground of encampment at five o'clock on the morning of the 13th October, in a single column by files from the right, and directed their march towards Arrah. The field officer of the day, Major Champion, with two hundred of the irregular cavalry, the troop of Hussars, and two companies of Grenadier Sepoys, with the quartermaster serjeants and camp-colour men of the several corps, formed the advanced guard. Just as the day began to dawn, the advance-guard having passed the bridge at Arrah, a famous partisan of Sujah Dowlah's lay in ambush with a select body of horse. He suffered the front to pass; but when the center had got opposite he rushed out upon them, cutting down all before him, and throwing the whole into the utmost confusion. Little resistance was made, every man shifting for himself by recovering the bridge, or swimming across the nulla; and most of them effected it under cover of the fire of the Sepoy grenadiers. These two companies were commanded by a subaltern officer, whose name the writer is sorry he cannot now recollect. He had not crossed the nulla, and, therefore, as soon as he perceived what had happened in front, he drew up his men at the foot of the bridge on the side next the army, and, as the enemy advanced, threw in a close fire, which drove them back, and favoured the escape of our friends. On the firing being heard in the rear, the King's battalion pushed on to support the advance, but it was all over before they got up. In this unfortunate business their loss was thirteen or fourteen Europeans, chiefly of the Hussars, and a good many of the irregulars. Here the writer cannot avoid mentioning the gallantry and presence of mind of Quarter-Master Serjeant Bennett, of the 89th Highland regiment, who, being mounted on a tattoo, had crossed the bridge, when seeing the confusion the advance was thrown into, attempted to regain it, but being singled out by one of the enemy armed with a spear, he despaired of being able to get off. He therefore drew his broad sword, determined to have at least a chance for his life. Fortunately for him the trooper's horse was rather unruly, and came up with him on the off side of Bennett, so that he could not use his spear. He instantly drew up, in order to bring the horse round, and coming very near, the Serjeant made a blow at him, with his sword, which cut the near rein, and brought the horse round the contrary way, which gave Bennett an opportunity to escape.

This check obliged the army to move with more caution. The European Grenadiers, with four companies of Grenadier Sepoys, were ordered in future to head the line, followed by the King's battalion; but the enemy's horse hung upon their flanks, and gave them a great deal of trouble, making a shew of attacking the advance, whenever they saw an opportunity, which obliged them frequently to halt, and unlimber their guns; but a few rounds

always sent them off. At last on the 22d
of October, about nine o'clock in the
morning, the advanced-guard entered the
plains of Buxar, where they perceived the
whole of Sujah Dowlah's army drawn out
to receive them, and about three miles in
their front. As the advance and King's
battalion entered the plain, they inclined
to the right towards the river, in order to
leave room for the several corps to form as
they came up. The enemy saluted them
with a few shot, which fell short, and after
looking at each other for more than an
hour Sujah Dowlah withdrew within his
lines. The camp equipage being come
up, the tents were pitched, and the troops
retired to them with positive orders not to
undress or take off their accoutrements.
As there was a village about a thousand
yards in front of the line, a battalion of
Sepoys was thrown into it to watch the
motions of the enemy.

Shortly after a Council of War was held, when it was determined not to attack the enemy until the morning of the 24th, that the troops might have full time to rest themselves. In the mean time all the heavy baggage was sent on board the boats.

Sujah Dowlah, not agreeing in opinion with the Council of War, put his army in motion early in the morning of the 23d, and when the commander in chief, with the field officer of the day, were going out to take a view of the enemy, they discovered them in full march to give them battle. The drums instantly beat to arms, and by eight o'clock the whole were formed in the order which had been laid down. On the right was a battalion of Sepoys, with two guns on its right, and two on its left;—then the King's battalion, with two guns on its left;—then a battalion of Se-

Battle of Buxar, 23d October, 1764.

poys, with two guns. On the left of these guns was the Bombay detachment, consisting of something more than one hundred Europeans, and Topasses, that is, native Portugueze dressed as Europeans, who formed the center and rear ranks. To the left of them were two guns, and upon the left of the whole a battalion of Sepoys, which, with two guns, completed the front line.

The second line was composed of three Sepoy battalions, and the Company's European battalion, with eight guns in the intervals. A battalion on each flank closed the square: that on the left had two guns attached to it. All the cavalry were drawn up on the left of the square—the lines about two hundred yards from each other. Major Champion commanded the right wing of the front line; Major Stibbert the left, and Major Pemble the rear line. Major Jennings, Commandant of Artillery, took post on the right.

By this time Sujah Dowlah's line had advanced within about five hundred yards of us, where they seemed to halt, and then we had a distinct view of them, and a grand sight it was: their left was close to the river, and their right extended into the country almost as far as the eye could carry, but bending a little inward, so as to bring their guns to bear on the left face of our square. About nine o'clock we began to advance upon the enemy, and then, for the first time, our fire opened, which we could clearly see had a fine effect. After moving about one hundred yards, a jeel,* in front of the left wing, obliged us to incline to the right in order to clear it. This took us up near an hour, the enemy's cannon and rockets playing upon us the whole

* Lake, swamp, or morass.

time; but their guns were not well served, otherwise, from the number they had in the field, they must have torn us to pieces.

The left having cleared the jeel, orders came along the line to move forward; but at that instant, a large body of cavalry appearing in the rear, obliged us to halt, and the rear line to go to the right about. The enemy's horse having been thrown into some disorder in coming through a village about a thousand yards in our rear, it took them a few minutes to close, and then they made a furious charge on the rear line; but they met with so warm a reception, both of grape and small arms, that they fled, and never after returned to the field. They took care, however, to carry off our baggage, and all the tents which had been left standing.

Whilst the rear line was engaged, the right wing of the enemy had bent round, so as nearly to inclose our left, and then the action in that quarter became warm. It was now about noon, when Major Munro rode to the right, and finding it much annoyed by a battery in a tope, or grove of trees, in front of the King's battalion, he ordered Major Stibbert's battalion, from the right of the line, to advance and attack it in flank. The battalion accordingly moved forward in excellent order; but receiving the fire of a battalion of Nejeebs,* and being attacked at the same time by a body of horse on each flank, they were thrown into disorder and retired towards the line. Major Munro having gone to the left, Major Champion ordered the right wing to advance, but not to give their fire until they could push bayonets: they accordingly moved on with recovered arms, and when they got in a line with

* Corps of infantry armed with matchlocks and sabres.

the disordered battalion, it instantly formed, and went on with them. On entering
the tope they received a heavy fire from
the Nejeebs, which, however, did little
execution. They pushed on, and on getting clear of the trees, perceiving the
Nejeebs had retreated, they gave them
their fire, which obliged them to quicken
their pace. At the back of the tope they
found twenty-seven pieces of cannon, some
of which had been taken from us at the
unfortunate affair at Manjee the year before. As soon as the guns were taken possession of, and the wing had reloaded,
they faced to the left, in order to support
the left wing and flank, still closely engaged; but the enemy, perceiving them
moving down, fled in disorder, so that at
one o'clock we were complete masters of
the field. The wing immediately halted,
and then Major Munro came in front of

the line, and returned thanks to the whole
army for their steadiness and bravery during the action ; after which, taking off his
hat, he gave three cheers for the victory,
which was returned by the troops with
hearty goodwill.

The line was once more put in motion,
in pursuit of the enemy ; but a large body
of cavalry being left to cover their retreat,
we were obliged to march with caution,
lest these fellows should break through
us, as they did at Arrah, so that we did
not reach the Tory Nulla until sunset.
Here a most horrid spectacle was presented
to us : Sujah Dowlah, when he advanced
to the field in the morning, left his camp
and bazar standing, not doubting but he
should gain an easy victory ; but when his
army gave way the bazar people ran towards the Nulla in order to cross it, but
the bottom being miry, and thousands of

people pushing in at the same time, with bullocks, horses, camels, and elephants, the whole became jammed together, and perished by the weight of each other, so that for an extent of nearly three hundred yards a complete bridge was formed. We turned from this dreadful sight, and took up our ground near the Fort of Buxar, where we lay on our arms all night.

Next morning, when the returns were collected, it was found that our loss in killed and wounded amounted to one hundred and one Europeans; seven hundred and seventy-three Sepoys, and about one hundred and forty or fifty of the irregular cavalry, making in the whole something more than one thousand men; but a vast number of our followers were killed and wounded between the lines. We lost but few officers, for, indeed, we had not many to lose, there being scarcely fifty, including all ranks, in the field. Lieutenant Spilsbury of the 96th regiment, and Ensign Thompson of the Grenadiers, to which, at his own request, he was appointed the evening before, were killed. Lieutenant George Thompson lost a leg, and Captain Crofton of the 96th, with three or four other officers, whose names cannot now be recollected, were slightly wounded.

We took in the field, and in the camp, one hundred and twenty-six pieces of cannon; and a foreigner, who had deserted from us at Sant, brought in, the day after the action, seven field pieces, which had been left in his charge, for which he received his pardon. Several of those deserters were found dead in the field, and two, who had been wounded, and could not get off with their army, were hung up to a tree in front of the line, by the provost serjeant.

Thus ended the battle of Buxar, on the issue of which depended the fate of Bengal. All the Native troops behaved to admiration, although some of them were new corps, not having been raised more than eight months. As to the Europeans, they were tried men, and enured to service.

Sujah Dowlah's army was reported to be nearly fifty thousand strong; and it was supposed his loss must have been considerable, as he never after faced us in the field.

.We halted at Buxar the three following days, during which time the bildars, or pioneers, were employed in burying the dead of both armies, and the dooly bearers in bringing off the wounded, many of the poor fellows having lain on the field for more than four and twenty hours for want of conveyance to bring them off:

as nearly half of the bearers ran away on the commencement of the action, and a number had been killed or disabled between the lines, there were not doolies sufficient to bring off with the army more than one fifth of the wounded.

On the 27th we marched back to the bank of the river, near the field of battle, and from thence crossed over into the Gauzipore district. The following day we took up our line of march towords Benares, and continued it every day until we reached the Goomty river, where we met the Emperor Shah Allum, who had quitted Sujah Dowlah, and once more threw himself on the generosity of the English. During one of these marches, just as we had come to our ground, the whole atmosphere was suddenly darkened, and a shower or cloud of locusts fell upon us, and covered the plain so thickly, that we were obliged to strike our bells of arms and colour tents, and move on to a spot of ground about four miles farther.

The Emperor accompanied us to Benares, which we found deserted by the enemy; we therefore marched round the city, and encamped on the plain near Murwaddee. Here we lay nearly two months, during which time all the public property belonging to Sujah Dowlah, which was found in the city, was sold by public auction, at the head of the army, for the benefit of the captors. About the middle of November a detachment was made, consisting of the Grenadiers, and three battalions of Sepoys, (whose names or numbers the writer cannot now recollect,) under the command of Major Pemble, to reduce the Fort of Chunar; but on attempting to storm it they were beaten back, and the detachment returned to the army.

Shortly after the army was reinforced by three hundred European recruits, and a battalion of Sepoys under Captain Ironside, then Town Major. This detachment had left Calcutta under the command of Major Sir Robert Fletcher, just arrived from England; and when he began his march, was led to believe that the Grand Army would not move until he had reached Patna; however, on hearing that Major Munro was advancing towards the enemy, without waiting for him, he quitted the detachment, and came on by dawk, or post, but did not get up with the army until the day after the battle. On his arrival Major Champion quitted the army, being appointed to command two companies of European recruits, and two battalions of Sepoys, in the provinces of Midnapore and Jellasore, to keep an eye upon the Maharattas, who were then in motion to assist Sujah Dowlah.

In the month of December all the King's troops were ordered to Calcutta, except those who chose to remain in the service of the Company; and about the 11th of January, 1765, Major Munro himself left the army, the command of which devolved on Sir Robert Fletcher. He immediately put the troops in motion. A strong detachment was formed for the reduction of Chunar, under the command of Major Stibbert, and, with the rest of the army, he marched against Allahabad, which after a few days siege was surrendered; and Major Stibbert, having also succeeded against Chunar, the army again united on the plain near Allahabad.

Early in the month of March Major Carnac, who had just been appointed a

Brigadier General from home, repaired to the army; and the Maharattas having about the same time entered the Doab, on the invitation of Sujah Dowlah, he marched to meet them, and after two slight actions drove them across the Jumna. Sujah Dowlah's affairs now became desperate: he therefore determined to follow the example of Shah Allum, for which purpose he repaired to the British camp, and threw himself on the mercy of the English Government, who granted him much better terms than he could have expected, which put an end to the war; after which the army fell back to Juanpore, not far from Benares, where it remained until Lord Clive joined it in the beginning of August. His Lordship then divided the troops into three brigades, as has been already noticed. The Mathews battalion being appointed to the 2d, the whole of that brigade, under Colonel Richard Smith, marched for Allahabad, the only fortress taken from Sujah Dowlah which we kept possession of—Chunar was restored to him. The first brigade, commanded by General Carnac, moved down to Monghyr; and the third, under Sir Robert Barker, united at Bankypore.

In 1766 the second brigade, being relieved by the third, the Mathews battalion, then commanded by Captain John Smith, a brother of the General's, was ordered to Benares, where it remained three or four years.

In 1770 it was ordered to the Presidency, where it was again relieved by the third brigade in 1772, when it was sent to Berhampore, then under the command of Captain Philip Delafield. In the latter end of 1773 the second brigade relieved the first, then in the field; and early in 1774 the whole of the second brigade. (except the Mathews battalion, which was ordered to Chunar) marched against the Rohillas; the brigade was under the command of Colonel Galliez; but Colonel Champion, being Commander in Chief, was at the head of the whole. In 1775, on General Clavering's arrangement taking place, the Mathews became the tenth in number, and the following year was ordered to Midnapore, where shortly after its arrival, great discontents broke out amongst the men, owing to intemperate and impro-per conduct on the part of their command-ing officer, which brought on an inquiry, and in consequence Captain Delafield was dismissed the service, by the sentence of a Court Martial, February, 1777. Who succeeded him in the command the writer cannot now recollect. In 1781 it was regimented, and became the 4th in number; and the following year, some symptoms of a mutinous tendency appearing, it was broke the beginning of 1784.* Thus fell the Mathews battalion, a corps more highly spoken of during the twenty-six years it existed, than any battalion in the service; and at this day, if you meet any of the old fellows who formerly belonged to it, and ask them what corps they came from, they will erect their heads, and say, " Mathews Ka Phulton."

———

The 19th Battalion was raised in Calcutta by the Town Major, about the middle of the year 1764, and when completed was given to Captain Hill. In 1765 it accompanied Lord Clive to the army, and was shortly after sent to the Court of

* See the Supplement for some account of that mutiny.

Sujah Dowlah, where it remained several years. In 1767 a hint was given to Captain Hill, that he would be superseded by Captain Muir, whenever a promotion of field officers took place, in consequence of which he resigned the service, and the command of the battalion was given to Captain Harper, who was at that time one of General Smith's family.*

* As the cause of this intended supersession is not generally known, the following account of it may not be unacceptable.

Captain Douglas Hill was the son of a gentleman in Ireland, who losing his father when very young, and his mother marrying again, he ran away from school in the year 1754, being then about fourteen years of age, and joined a recruiting party of the 39th regiment, commanded by Colonel Aldercorn, and then under orders for the East Indies. Being too young to carry arms he was made a drummer, and arrived with the regiment at Madras, in the year 1755, being the first British regiment that ever rounded the Cape of Good Hope. Early the following year two additional companies were sent out to the regiment, one of which was commanded by the late Lieutenant General Sir Eyre Coote. Calcutta having been taken by Surajah Dowlah, in June, 1756, four companies of Colonel Alder-

Captain Harper kept this battalion until 1773, when he resigned the service, and

corn's regiment were sent on board Admiral Watson's
fleet, to act as Marines, and to be employed on shore, if
necessary, for the recovery of our settlements—Captain
Coote's company, and the one Mr. Hill belonged to, were
in this detachment.

During the year 1757, the Company's possessions being
recovered by the overthrow and death of Surajah Dowlah,
the 39th regiment was ordered home the beginning of the
year 1758, allowing such officers and soldiers to enter into
the Company's service as chose to remain, promising to
the officers their half-pay for life. In consequence of this
assurance, the following officers came in with advanced
rank, viz. Major Ford as Lieutenant Colonel; Lieutenants
Carnac* and York† as Captains; and Ensigns Donnellan‡
and Bradbridge as Lieutenants, and almost the whole of
the Non-commissioned Officers and Privates. Captain

* Afterwards a Brigadier General and Commander in
Chief.

† Was Town Major of Fort William.

‡ This unfortunate man was executed at Warwick in
1781, for the supposed murder of his brother-in-law, Sir
Theodosius Boughton. He was condemned on the evi-
dence of his mother-in-law, who, through remorse, on her
death bed, confessed that she had administered the poison
herself, which deprived her son of life, and declared Mr.
Donnellan to be innocent.

the temporary command of it was given
to Captain Robert Stuart, (now Lieutenant

Coote went home with the colours, and Mr. Hill embarked in the same ship.   During the voyage, Captain Coote,
perceiving him to be a smart youth, and in appearance far
above his situation, inquired who he was, and, to his
astonishment, discovered him to be the son of an old and
intimate friend.   He immediately took the young man,
then about eighteen, under his own protection, and, on
their arrival in England, procured his discharge.

In December, 1758, the Court of Directors having represented to Government, that a regiment of Europeans
was absolutely necessary for the protection of their settlements in Bengal, his Majesty was pleased to order one to
be formed by drafts from the old corps, purposely for that
duty, and, at the recommendation of the Court, Captain
Coote was appointed to the command of it, with the
rank of Lieutenant Colonel Commandant, and the regiment was numbered the Eighty-fourth.   To this regiment
Mr. Hill was appointed Quarter-master, his warrant bearing date the 7th of February, 1759.

The regiment arrived at Madras the latter end of the
year 1759, and their services being required on the coast,
they were immediately disembarked, when Colonel Coote
became the Commander in Chief.   The first vacant commission was given to Mr. Hill.   The power of the French,
in the Carnatic, being entirely ruined by the capture of
Pondicherry, Colonel Coote, in 1761, embarked his regiment for Bengal, in two large country ships, one of

General,) who was ordered to proceed
with it to join its brigade, then at the Pre-

which, the Fatty Islam, foundered near the Sand Heads, and
almost every soul perished. The regiment was completed
by drafts of men from home; but the promotion of officers
went on in the corps. This brought Mr. Hill very high on
the list of Lieutenants.

In 1763 the regiment was actively employed during the
whole of that severe campaign, in which it acquired much
honour, and at the conclusion of it were ordered home, allowing to the officers and men the same terms as had been
granted to Colonel Aldercorn's regiment. In consequence
of this Lieutenants Goddard, Fielding, Neilson, Hill, and
Comine, came in as Captains. Ensigns Auchmuty, Roper,
Knudson, Skinner, Camac, and Robinson, as Lieutenants;
all their commissions dated in the month of October, 1763.
Here we will leave Mr. Hill and speak of Captain Muir.

Captain Grainger Muir was the son of a respectable
officer in his Majesty's service, who was one of the majors
sent out in command of twelve Independent Companies in
Admiral Boscawen's fleet, in the year 1747, in order, if
possible, to recover Madras, and some other settlements,
which had been taken from the Company the year before
by the French, and Mr. Muir, then a youth about fourteen,
accompanied his father.

The Admiral arrived at Fort St. David's the latter end
of the year, and, with the assistance of the garrison of that
place, invested Pondicherry; but the Monsoon setting in,
and some mismanagement having existed in the engineer de-

sidency; but on his arrival at Patna, he
found orders for him to cross the Ganges,

partment, he was obliged to raise the siege, with considerable loss. He sat down against it a second time in
1748, but had made little progress, when accounts were
received from England of a general peace. Madras being
restored by the treaty, the troops moved from Pondicherry
to take possession of it, where Major Muir died the following year. Young Mr. Muir remained at Madras until
the year 1752, when the Court of Directors appointed him
a writer on the Bengal Establishment. On his arrival in
Calcutta, he was appointed to an office; but disliking the
inactivity of the situation, he solicited the Governor and
Council to grant him permission to resign it, and indulge
him with a commission in the army. His request was
accordingly complied with, and an Ensign's commission
given him in the year 1754.

In 1756, when Surajah Dowla took the Fort of Calcutta,
where so many of our countrymen suffered in the Black
Hole, Ensign Muir was stationed with twenty men at the
factory of Jugdia, under the orders of Mr. Amyat, the
Chief, with Messrs. Pleydell, Verelst, Smyth, and Hay, of
the Civil Service. They were directed by the Governor
and Council to quit the factory, and repair to Fulta, where
the dispersed English were collecting, under the protection
of some of the Company's ships, just arrived from Europe.

On the arrival of Colonel Clive and Admiral Watson,
with reinforcements from Madras, the army was ordered

and scour the country through the districts of Purnea, Dinagepore, Rungpore,

to take the field; when Mr. Muir was made a Captain, and as such, commanded a company at the battle of Plassey, as he did in every other action during the year 1757. In the following year, a Captain Gowen, of the Bombay Establishment, came round to Bengal, and being an old officer, Colonel Clive gave him a Majority in this army. This gave so much dissatisfaction to the Bengal officers, that eight Captains resigned their commissions in one day: these were Rumbold, (afterwards Sir Thomas,) Alexander Grant, Muir, Carstairs and Campbell;* the names of the other three the writer cannot now recal to his memory. Captain Muir repaired to England, and in January, 1760, procured a Lieutenancy in the 94th Regiment, with which he served in America the remainder of the seven years' war. In 1763 the Regiment was disbanded.

The

* These two gentlemen were afterwards restored to the service, but with loss of rank. Captain Rumbold applied at the same time, but was refused, on a supposition that he was a leading man in the resignation; he was, however, in the year 1760, appointed to the Civil Service, and, with a number of other gentlemen, sent out as Factors on the Bengal Establishment. Captain Grant returned to Bengal as a free merchant, and died in 1765—then Contractor for the army.

and Cooss Behar, then much infested by
the Sanasses. He executed his orders

The latter end of the same year, accounts having reached
England of the war with Cossim Ally, and the destruction
of the Patna detachment, proposals were made to some of
the disbanded Lieutenants to raise men for Bengal, on the
Company's bounty, which was five guineas, and those who
could enlist one hundred and twenty-five were to have
Captains' commissions. Many offered their service, and
amongst the rest Lieutenant Muir, who soon completed
his company, and with it embarked for India; but having
a long passage, did not arrive in Bengal until early in 1765.
He was immediately sent off to join the army, where he
had the mortification to find Captain Hill, who was so
much his junior at the battle of Plassey eight years before,
now his senior officer. He represented to Lord Clive the
very unpleasant predicament in which he was placed, and
entreated his Lordship to relieve him from it. But Lord
Clive told him that Captain Hill was an officer of very considerable merit, and he would not on any account allow him
to be superseded. However, in January, 1767, Lord
Clive quitted Bengal, and Mr. Verelst, the friend of Captain Muir, succeeding him, things took a different turn,
and the hint before mentioned was the consequence.

On the resignation of Captain Hill, he returned to England, where he remained a few years, and was afterwards
restored to the service, but was drowned coming from
Madras in the year 1777.

F 2   Cap-

most effectually, which in a great measure
broke the spirits of those troublesome marauders, as they have been tolerably quiet
ever since. The battalion remained in
Cooss Behar, where Captain John Fullarton
(late a Major-General) took the command
of it.

In 1775, on General Clavering's arrangement taking place, it became the 20th in
number; and shortly after was ordered,
with the rest of the brigade, to relieve the
2d brigade, then cantoned at Belgram, in
the province of Oude, where it remained
until the latter end of the year 1777, when
it marched to the Presidency.

In 1778, Captain Fullarton having been
promoted to a Majority, Captain Peter
Grant was appointed to the command of

Captain Muir lived to attain the rank of full Colonel,
and died on his way to England in the year 1785.

it ; and war with France breaking out the same year, the late Lieutenant-Colonel Dow, with this and another battalion, was ordered to take possession of Chandernagore, when the public property found in the place was given to the captors. In 1781, it was formed into a regiment, and ordered to the coast ; but on its arrival at Midnapore, a dispute arose between Captain (then Major) Grant and his men, concerning the distribution of the Chandernagore prize money, when the battalion mutinied, for which it was broke, and the men drafted into the other five regiments then under orders for the Carnatic. The Major was tried and cashiered.

The 24th Battalion was raised at Bankypore in the year 1766, under the direction of the late Sir Robert Barker, and when it was disciplined, was turned over to the Purgunnah Establishment at Patna. The latter end of the year it was given to Captain Jacob Camac, who was ordered with it to Ramgur, where it remained many years. On the reduction of the Purgunnah Establishment in 1773, this was the only battalion that was allowed to remain; and in 1775, by General Clavering's arrangement, it was brought into the line, posted to the 2d brigade, and became the Fourteenth in number. In 1778, Captain Camac was promoted to a Majority, and Captain James Brown succeeded him in the command. The following year it was ordered into the Maharatta country, with some other corps under the command of Major (afterwards Lieutenant Colonel) Camac, where it served with great credit. When Captain Brown left this battalion, or who succeeded him in the command of it, the writer cannot now recollect. When the battalions of the first brigade returned from Bombay, an alteration took place in the number of the battalions, when this became the Fifteenth.

In the beginning of 1788, Captain Ludovic Grant was appointed to the command of it; but no opportunity of service offered until the end of 1795, when the Government had it in contemplation to send a detachment by sea, to the settlement of Malacca, and it was understood that this battalion had volunteered to be employed on that duty. However, when the men learnt that they were actually to embark on board ship, a serious mutiny broke out, and Major-General Erskine was ordered down to Midnapore to quell it. On their refusing to lay down their arms, he brought Captain Bradley's bat-

talion, then at the same station, with its
field-pieces, against them, and after a few
shot dispersed the mutineers, and they
fled in every direction. No blame was
imputed to Captain Grant and his officers,
so far from it, that Government ordered
another battalion to be raised by them,
which was just completed, when the present Establishment took effect.

Having given an account of the four old battalions which have been reduced, the corps remaining in the service will be treated of as they stand in regiments by the arrangement of 1796.

FIRST REGIMENT—

was composed of the 1st, 13th and 32d battalions.

First Battalion.—This corps was raised at Burdwan in the year 1758, and still retains the name of that province. By whom it was raised, or where employed until the year 1763, the writer cannot now recollect. In the latter end of that year it joined the marines at Burdwan, and accompanied them along the Maharatta frontier, towards Ramgur, as has been already mentioned. It afterwards proceeded to the army with the Madras detachment, and joined it a little before the mutiny. It was then commanded by Captain M'Lean, and in April, 1764, it became the Second in number.

In the action with Sujah Dowla, before Patna, on the 3d May, it acquitted itself with much credit; but in consequence of a representation from the Native Officers, Captain M'Lean was removed, and Captain Nollikins, who was wounded at the head of the European Grenadiers that day, was appointed to it in his room. It accompanied the grand army to Buxar, and in that action was, to the best of the writer's recollection, on the left of the front line. Its captain had been left sick at Patna, but whether it was commanded by Lieutenants Bevan or Harper he cannot now tell, as both those gentlemen were made Majors of Brigade by Lord Clive, for their gallant behaviour in that battle.

It remained with the grand army until the war with Sujah Dowla was concluded, and was, in 1765, posted to the first brigade, and accompanied it to Monghyr. In 1766, it was turned over to the Purgunnah establishment and sent to Maradbaug, being then commanded by Captain Fischer, where it remained until 1773, when it was ordered to join its brigade.

In 1775, it became the First in number; and, in the year 1778, was one of the battalions ordered to Bombay under Colonel Leslie first, and afterwards under the command of General Goddard, where its behaviour was highly to the satisfaction of its commander. It returned to Bengal in 1784, with Colonel (now Lieut. General) Charles Morgan, where it has remained ever since.* Captain (since Major Gene-

---

* It was in Rohilcund with General Abercrombie, in 1794, and was the right battalion of the centre brigade,

ral) Forbes commanded this corps on the march towards Bombay. On his promotion Captain John Campbell succeeded to the command, which he retained with distinction to himself and the corps during the greater part of the war: after him Major James Dickson commanded it.

Second Battalion.—This has been long a distinguished battalion. It was raised at Midnapore about the year 1759, and continued some years in that province, from which it took its name. In 1764 it was commanded by Captain (late Colonel) Hampton, and became the Fourteenth in number, according to his rank. In 1765 it was posted to the third brigade, and the

commanded by Lieutenant Colonel Ware. Captain Robert Baillie was then at the head of it. Its loss was trifling in the action of the 26th October of that year, fought on the plains of Bætoorah.

following year was turned over to the Purgunnah or Provincial Establishment. On
the reduction of that Establishment in
1773, it was ordered to join its brigade at
Berhampore, where Captain (late Colonel)
Blane got the command of it, and this officer having the entire disciplining of it,
(after being so long broken by detachments in the Mofusseil,) and being obliged
to exchange a number of the men, it has
ever since gone by his name. By the
regulations of General Clavering in 1775,
it became the Nineteenth in number, and
the following year accompanied its brigade to Belgram in the province of Oude.
In 1778 it marched down to the Presidency, where it remained until January,
1781, when it was ordered to the coast.
It was at the same time formed into a regiment of two battalions, and Major Blane
again placed at the head of it, when it

became the Thirteenth in number, which it has ever since retained. During the whole of the war on the coast the conduct of this excellent corps was highly spoken of, but particularly at the attack of the lines of Cuddalore on the 13th of June, 1783. At the latter end of the following year it returned to Bengal, and being then attached to the first brigade, accompanied it to Cawnpore in January, 1786, where it remained until the beginning of 1788, when it returned to the Presidency, being then commanded by Captain Norman M'Leod. In 1790 it was again ordered to the coast, and as usual acquitted itself much to the satisfaction of that excellent judge of merit—the late Marquis Cornwallis. On the 6th of February, 1792, when his Lordship attacked the lines of Tippoo Sultan, this battalion was in the right column with Lieutenant Colonel Cockerell,

under the command of Major General
Meadows, where they had a smart action
with the French party commanded by a
M. Law or Lally. On the evening of
that day, notwithstanding it had been under arms and in movement all the preceding night, it was selected by the Commander in Chief to accompany one of the
European regiments to beat up the quarters of the enemy's cavalry, then encamped
under the walls of Seringapatam, which
they fully executed. It returned to Bengal in 1793, when it was ordered to its old
station at Cawnpore.

In 1794, it was again in motion, under
the command of Captain N. M'Leod, and
ordered into Rohilcund, in consequence of
some misunderstanding with the Rohilla
chiefs, where Major General Sir Robert
Abercrombie took the command of the
army, which consisted of the Second Eu-

ropean Regiment, ten battalions of Sepoys, and two weak regiments of Native cavalry, with a proportion of Artillery. This battalion, with the 18th, commanded by Major Bolton, and the Second European Regiment, formed the reserve, under Colonel Burrington, assisted by Major Macdonald: the 13th on the right; the Europeans in the centre, and the 18th on the left. Having advanced into the enemy's country near Rampore, the Rohilla chiefs boldly marched out to meet them, and in the morning of the 26th October, they took up a commanding position about a mile in front of the British camp. The army was instantly formed in one line, with the reserve on the right, and its flank covered by the cavalry, which formed an angle, so as to protect the rear. The centre was commanded by Colonel Ware, and the left by Lieutenant-Colonel M'Gowan;

each with four battalions.* The 10th battalion, being on the left of the line, was ordered to the rear, to protect the baggage; and the next battalion upon the left, being the 14th, commanded by Captain Hyndman, fell back and formed an angle to cover that flank. As soon as the line was formed, the whole advanced upon the enemy; but the reserve moved forward with so rapid a pace, that the guns attached to it could not keep up, and consequently were left in the rear. At this time the enemy were concealed in the jungle, not only in front, but on both flanks. When the line halted, some orders were sent to the cavalry, which, it seems, were not clearly understood. The officer commanding them, Captain Ramsay, how-ever, directed them to wheel to the *left*

---

* The two divisions commanded by Colonel Forbes.

G

by divisions, which, being perceived by
the Rohilla horse, they dashed upon them
full speed, and in less than a minute, the
two regiments fled in confusion, breaking
in upon, and disordering the 13th battalion as they went off. In this situation,
Captain M'Leod called to his people to
fire upon them, but it was too late, for the
enemy's horse and foot were on him in a
moment; and the battalion being much
broken by our own cavalry, could make but
little resistance, so that the Rohillas had nothing to do but cut down, and a dreadful
slaughter it was—every officer in the battalion being either killed or wounded, and
full one third of the men. Captain M'Leod
was the first who fell. The enemy nearly
at the same time fell upon the right wing
of the European battalion, which was
handled very roughly, and lost many officers and men. The 18th battalion did

not escape. The attack upon it was also on the right, where Major Bolton lost his life. During this transaction, Lieutenant Gahan, (now Lieutenant-Colonel,) and Lieutenant Richardson, (now of the Civil Service,) having rallied some of the cavalry, returned to the field, and assisted in dispersing the enemy.

The Rohillas made an attempt on the left flank, but there they could make no impression, Captain Hyndman being prepared for them. After this they were soon routed, and driven from the field.

The army lost a number of excellent officers upon this occasion.

The Rohillas retired to the hills, where the Commander in Chief followed them, and, at last, prevailed on them to lay down their arms, after which the troops returned to their cantonments.

In 1796, it came into this regiment.

The *32d battalion*, which was incorporated with the two before-mentioned, was one of the new battalions formed in 1786 from the extra companies of the old corps; and as the companies from four battalions formed one on the new establishment, they were denominated by the Natives " Charri Yarie," or the Four Friends. This battalion was with Sir Robert Abercrombie against the Rohillas, in October, 1794, but being in the centre of the line did not suffer much.

SECOND REGIMENT

was formed from the 2d, 25th, and 28th Battalions.

First Battalion.—This is an old corps; and, if the writer is not mistaken, it was formerly called the Chittagong Battalion; but it has long since lost that name, and now goes by the denomination of " Grant," from Colonel Hugh Grant, who when a Captain long commanded it.

It was raised in the year 1759, but where or by whom cannot now be recollected.

Captain Grant got the command of it in 1761, and remained with it at Chandernagore, until the war with Cossim Ally broke out, when it joined the army under Major Adams, and continued actively employed during the whole contest. After the retreat of Sujah Dowla from Patna, this battalion was sent to Moneah to watch the motions of the enemy, where it remained during all the rains, until the army joined it from Bankypore. It was one of the first battalions that crossed the Soane with the Grenadiers, after which it accompanied the army to Buxar, and in that action had the right of the second line, where its behaviour was steady and soldier-like.

When the battalions were numbered in April, 1764, it became, by the rank of its Captain, the Third.

At the conclusion of the war in 1765, it was posted to the 1st Brigade, and ordered to Monghyr.

In 1767, war breaking out with Hyder Ally, this was one of three battalions sent to the Northern Sircars under the command of Lieut. Colonel Wm. Smith, who died shortly after, and then Colonel Peach, with a part of his Regiment, (the 1st Europeans,) was sent round to take the command. The battalion was then under the orders of Captain Arthur Forbes Auchmuty.

It returned to Bengal in the latter end

of 1769, and was ordered up to Dinapore, where its brigade was then stationed. In 1772 the whole of the first brigade was ordered to the field to oppose the Maharattas, who had entered the Doab, but retired on the approach of the brigade. The following year it was again sent without the provinces, but nothing occurred, after which it was ordered to the Presidency.

In 1775, when General Clavering's alteration took effect, it became the Second in number: and in 1778 was one of the six battalions sent to Bombay, under the command of the late General Goddard, where its conduct was highly to the satisfaction of the General, and particularly in the retreat from the Ghauts in 1781. In 1784 it returned to Bengal, where it remained until it became incorporated in the Second Regiment. This corps, on the march towards Bombay, was commanded by Captain Popham; Captain Solomon Earle succeeded Captain Popham, and commanded it during the greater part of the war. Major Maitland then commanded, and returned with it to Bengal.

Second Battalion.—This Battalion was raised at Cawnpore in the year 1778, by Captain Charles Bowles, whose name it still bears. It was ordered to the Presidency in 1780, and early the following year was formed into a regiment, and numbered the 25th; after which it marched to the coast under the late Colonel Pearse, where it acquitted itself with much credit during that arduous contest with Hyder Ally, and after his death with his son Tippoo Sultan.

In the beginning of 1785, it returned to Bengal, where it remained until 1796, when it was placed in the 2d Regiment.

The 28*th*, which was divided between the two before-mentioned battalions, was one of those formed for the service of the Vizier in 1776; and being first commanded by Captain John Landeg, it retained his name. It served in the Maharatta country under the late Colonel Muir in 1781-2; after which it returned within the provinces. In 1790, it was one of those ordered to the coast under the command of the late Colonel Cockerell, where it served during the whole of that war, and in 1793 returned to Bengal.

On its marching to Madras, it was commanded by Captain Scrimgeour, who died at Bangalore in 1791, and was succeeded by Captain Thomas Welsh.

THIRD REGIMENT

was formed from the 3d, 22d, and 27th Battalions.

First Battalion.—This is an old corps, and one of those formed in the early part of the service; but when, or by whom, the writer cannot now recollect. In 1764 it was commanded by Captain Campbell, and, agreeably to his rank, became the Fourth in number. In 1765 it was posted to the first brigade, and marched to Monghyr. In 1767, being then commanded by Captain Clotworthy Gowan, (whose name it still retains,) it was ordered to the Northern Sircars under the late Lieutenant Colonel William Smith, where it remained until 1769, when it returned to Bengal.

In 1775, on General Clavering's regulation being put in force, it became the

Third in number; and when the first brigade of Sepoys was ordered to Bombay in 1778 under General Goddard, this was the only battalion of that brigade which was not ordered on that service; it was then commanded by Captain Allan Macpherson, and was on duty in Chunar. The beginning of 1781 it was formed into a regiment, and became the First in number; but on the return of the battalions from the west of India, it was again pushed back to its present standing.

In 1790 it was ordered to the coast, and was then commanded by the late Captain Sir Patrick Balfour; it served there during the whole of the war against Tippoo Saheb, and returned to Bengal in 1793. In 1796 it was formed into this regiment.

Second Battalion.—This corps is one of

the battalions formed for the Vizier, by British officers, in 1776, and was afterwards taken into the Company's service. It was considered as an excellent battalion, although it had no opportunity of distinguishing itself. It was first commanded by Captain Young, whose name it still bears.

The Twenty-seventh Battalion—which completed this regiment, was another of the Vizier's corps. It was called the Kallie Battalion, and stands nearly in the same situation, with respect to service, as the foregoing.

FOURTH REGIMENT

was formed from the 4th, 31st, and 37th Battalions.

First Battalion.—This corps was raised

in or about the year 1759, but by whom
the writer cannot recollect, nor does he
remember who commanded it in 1764,
when it became the Fifth in number. In
1765, it was under the command of a
Captain M'Pherson, who died the same
year, and was succeeded by Captain
Whichcott, who quitted it at the general
resignation in May, 1766. In 1768, Captain James Crawford, senior, got the
command of it, and it now bears his name.
By General Clavering's orders, in 1775,
it became the Fourth in number. It continued with its brigade all the following
years until 1778, when it was órdered to
Bombay, with five other battalions; and
a few days after its march from Culpee,
on the other side of the Jumna, it lost its
Captain, who was a very great favourite
of the corps. It continued on that service
during the whole of the war, and acquired

the character of a steady and excellent battalion.*   It returned to Bengal in 1784, and was not afterwards actively employed until it was incorporated in this regiment in 1796.

Second Battalion.—This corps was formed as Light Infantry, by Captain James Crawford, jun. in 1778, and intended for the duty of Ramgur, where it remained until the year 1786, when, as an Independent Corps, it was ordered to be reduced, and had actually marched towards Dinapore for that purpose; but before it reached the cantonments, orders for the new establishment arrived from Europe, and then it was brought into the line as the 31st battalion.   It still bears the name of its

* After Captain Crawford's death, the Senior Lieutenant, Archdeacon, continued in the command of this battalion, (which was considered the finest corps on that service,) until Major Dawes was appointed to it, from Bengal.

first Captain, and is, by way of distinction, called the " Choota (or 2d) Crawford."

The Thirty-seventh Battalion.—This battalion was just formed by Captain Ludowick Grant, to supply the place of the 15th, which had been reduced at Midnapore for mutiny.

1795

——————

FIFTH REGIMENT

was formed from the 5th, 23d, and 35th Battalions.

First Battalion.—This corps was raised in Calcutta in 1763, by Captain Gilbert Ironside, whose name it still retains. In 1764, it became the Tenth in number, according to the rank of its Captain ; and the latter end of the same year joined the grand army at Benares, then commanded by Major Munro. In 1765, it was posted to the First Brigade, and repaired with it to Monghyr. In 1767, Captain Bevan, who had been appointed a Major of Brigade by Lord Clive, for his good conduct at Buxar, got the command of it, which he kept for many years. In 1774, it was ordered to join the Second Brigade, then on its march into Rohilcund, and was present at the action with the Rohillas, which took place the 23d April, near the village of Tessunah; but the officers and soldiers call it the battle of St. George. In this action it acquitted itself with much gallantry, as indeed did the whole of the brigade with which it acted.

In 1775, it became the Fifth in number, in consequence of General Clavering's plan; and in 1778, marched to the west of India, under the command of Captain Gough, who fell at the head of it at the storm of Amadabad, the 15th of February, 1780. It served the whole of that war with distinction. Captain ———— succeeded Captain Gough for a while, after which Captain Robert (now Maj. Gen. Sir Robert) Blair was appointed to command this corps; then Major Harding, and Captain John Rattray, returned in command of it to Bengal, in 1784, where it was stationed until 1796, when it formed a part of this regiment.

Second Battalion.—This was one of the battalions formed for the service of the Vizier in 1776, and afterwards taken into the service of the Company. The writer does not think it was actively employed until it became attached to the 5th Regiment. It was first commanded by Captain Baillie, and retains that name.

The Thirty-fifth, which completed the two battalions before-mentioned, was one of the Charrie Yari Battalions, formed from old corps in 1786.

H

SIXTH REGIMENT

was formed from the 6th, 20th, and 36th battalions.

1st Battalion.—This is an old corps, and was raised about the year 1758; but how it was employed until the year 1763, the writer does not now recollect.

It was early in the field under Major Adams on the commencement of the war with Cossim Ally, being then commanded by Captain Swinton, who lost an arm some time before, but where the writer does not now remember. It goes by his name.

The conduct of this corps was highly spoken of during the whole of the war.

In April, 1764, it became the Thirteenth in number, and the following year was posted to the first brigade. It was one of the battalions sent to the Northern Sircars, in 1767, with Lieutenant Colonel William Smith, where it remained until the latter end of 1769. When General Clavering's regulations were put in force, it became the Sixth in number. In 1778 it was ordered to Bombay, being then commanded by Captain George Waugh, and on crossing the Jumna at Culpee, it was one of the battalions which were ordered to attack the lines thrown up there by the Maharattas, which they carried at the point of the bayonet. Major (afterwards General) Fullarton commanded the two battalions sent on that duty. Major Sinclair succeeded Captain Waugh in the command of this corps whilst on service under General Goddard. After him Captain Coleridge commanded, and returned with it to Bengal.

This battalion distinguished itself during the whole of those campaigns in common with the other corps on that long and arduous service.

It returned to Bengal in 1784, where it remained until 1794, when it was again put in motion against the Rohillas, and was present in the unfortunate action which took place on the 26th of October, but being in the centre of the line its loss was very trifling. It was then commanded by Captain P. Douglas, who held it until it came into the present regiment.

Second Battalion.—This corps was one of the battalions formed for the Vizier, by British officers, in 1776: and was afterwards incorporated in the service of the Company, and joined the temporary brigade. Its denomination was that of the Raje Battalion, which it still retains. It was in the battle of Bætoorah in Rohilcund, on the 26th October, 1794; but having been in the centre of the line did not sustain a single casualty.

The *36th Battalion*, which, with the other two, completed this regiment, was one of the Charrie Yari corps formed in 1786. In 1794 it formed part of the army in Rohilcund with Sir Robert Abercrombie; and in the action of the 26th October, being in the centre of the line, its loss was very trifling.*

========

SEVENTH REGIMENT

was composed of the 7th, 16th, and 24th battalions.

First Battalion.—This corps was raised at Mooshedabad early in 1764, by Captain Thomas Goddard, whose distinguished name it still bears; and before it received

---

* Whether this battalion was in that action, or left in charge of the cantonments of Cawnpoor, seems doubtful. If in the action, there must have been eleven Native battalions in the field.

its arms it was ordered to join the army in the field. In April, 1764, the Marines having arrived at Moorshedabad on their march to Patna, this battalion was directed to accompany them.

In 1764, when the rank of the several battalions was fixed, it became the 17th in number, and the following year was attached to the first brigade, with which it proceeded to Monghyr. In 1772, it was employed with the rest of the brigade to drive the Maharattas from Rohilcund, which they effected, and then returned to cantonments.

In 1775, on General Clavering's regulations taking effect, this battalion, being the youngest in the first brigade, became the Seventh in number.

In 1778, it accompanied its old captain (then Lieutenant Colonel Goddard) to the west of India, and at Culpee was one of

the battalions which attacked the Maharatta intrenchment under the command
of Major Fullarton.

During the greater part of that war it
was commanded by Captain D. Lucas,
and it amply did its duty upon every occasion on which it was employed, and
returned to Bengal with the other battalions in 1784. It was again in motion in
the year 1790, being ordered to the coast
under Colonel Cockerell. It was then
commanded by Captain John Rattray,
with whose conduct Lord Cornwallis was
highly pleased during those three arduous
campaigns. In 1793, it returned to its
brigade, and three years afterwards was
incorporated into the Seventh Regiment.

Second Battalion.—This is an old and
distinguished corps, and in the early part
of the service, there was scarcely an action

of any note in which it was not engaged.

Prior to the year 1763, the writer has not been able to recollect the names of its commanders, but in that year it was commanded by Captain Trevánion. It served with great credit the whole campaign under Major Adams; and when that officer left the army at Sant, this battalion shewed some symptoms of insubordination with the other troops, but were soon quieted by Captain Trevanion, who was much beloved by his men.* It accompanied Major Carnac to Buxar, and afterwards to Patna, where its behaviour in the action which took place on the 3d of May, 1764, was highly meritorious.

* His memory, in connexion with that of the corps, and his conciliatory conduct in the command of it, was long cherished by the Native soldiery, under the appellation of Teerbænies Battalion—the Indian pronunciation of Trevanion.

About this time it became the Sixth in number, according to the rank of its Captain.

On the retreat of Sujah Dowla from Patna, it was one of the corps ordered to clear the Choprah district, under the command of Major Champion, which having effected, it cantoned near the town of Choprah on the setting in of the rains, which were very violent that year. In the month of September, on hearing that the battalion at Manjie had mutinied, and quitted their station, this battalion, with the Marines, were ordered after them, as has been already mentioned.

In October, 1764, this battalion and the Mathews accompanied the Marines until they joined the Grand Army near Arrah, on the 10th of that month. At the battle of Buxar it was in the front line, where its conduct was as usual. After the

action, Captain Trevanion left the battalion, being ordered to Calcutta by the
Governor and Council; and here the
writer hopes he will be excused in telling
the following anecdote regarding him.
On his way down he spent a day with
his old friend, Captain John White, who
then commanded at Monghyr, and after
dinner they took a walk to the Hill in the
Fort, on which the great house now stands,
and from which there is a most beautiful
prospect. He said to his friend, in a joke,
" that when he died, he should like to be
buried there." Having settled his business
with the Honourable Board, he was on
his way back to the field; but being taken
ill, he died the very day he arrived at
Monghyr Ghaut, which was the 25th of
December, 1764; when Captain White,
recollecting the spot he stood on at the
time he expressed the wish before-men-

tioned, ordered a grave to be prepared for him, where his bones now lie, under a plain stone, without an inscription, in front of the great house.

The command of the battalion was then given to Captain Duffield, who gave an entertainment to the Native officers and Sepoys on joining it, since which it has gone by his name. In 1765, it was posted to the Third Brigade, which at that time was composed of some of the finest corps, both European and Native, then in the service; but this was considered as a pattern battalion, next to the European regiment, with which Sir Robert Barker took a great deal of pains.

In 1768, that excellent officer, Captain John Jones, got the command of it; the brigade being then at Allahabad, from whence it marched to Dinapore the latter end of the following year, where it remained until January, 1771, when the whole brigade moved up to the Carumnassa, to be in readiness to take the field, in case the Maharattas entered the province of Allahabad, which was then apprehended; but they dropped the design. The brigade then marched to Buxar, where the Europeans embarked and dropped down to Monghyr, and were joined there by the Sepoys, who moved down by land. Here the brigade remained until February, 1772, when an invasion by the French was supposed to be in agitation, in consequence of some misunderstanding with the Court of Spain, regarding Falkland's Island. It was therefore ordered immediately to the Presidency, and on its arrival at Cowgatchy, opposite to Ghyretty, was directed to encamp; where it was shortly after joined by the Second Brigade, from Fort William.

In June, the brigades separated, the Second for Berhampore and Monghyr, and the Third for the Presidency. In the latter end of the same year, the Bootias, or inhabitants of Bootan, having overrun the province of Cooss Behar, this battalion was ordered out to clear it; and a hard and severe service it had of it. In April, 1773, at the storm of Delamcotta, one of the strongest forts in that district, a detachment of the battalion gained great honour. In advancing to the breach, where the Bootias were ready to receive them, the colour-man was killed, when the standard fell, and the men seemed to recoil; which being perceived by the late Mr. Harvey, then a Lieutenant in the battalion, he took it up and advanced to the breach, followed by his men, who were soon masters of the place.

In May, 1773, it had the misfortune to

lose its Captain, who was succeeded by Captain Skinner, but he also died in December the same year,* when Captain Gravely was appointed to the command of it; about which time it returned to its brigade, then at Berhampore.

In 1775, it became the Fifteenth in number, in consequence of General Clavering's arrangement. Shortly after, it accompanied the brigade to Dinapore, and afterwards to Belgram, in the province of Oude, where the whole cantoned in one line; the European regiment in the centre, with the Park of Artillery on its right, and three battalions of Sepoys on each flank. In 1776, the Vizier's troops were thrown into a state bordering on mutiny, in consequence of the appointment of

---

* Both those excellent officers fell victims to the unhealthy climate of Cooss Behar.

British officers to command them, and many of the chiefs refused to obey orders from court on that head. Amongst the rest, a man of considerable rank, named Mahboob-Khan, who rented the province of Korah, was one of the foremost. He had the command of a large body of Nejeebs, or Matchlocks, with a good park of artillery, and it was thought right to have a watchful eye over him. Colonel Parker was therefore detached with this, and the Sixteenth Battalion, commanded by Captain (now Lieutenant-General) William Jones, with four guns, in the month of May, to the city of Korah, near which it encamped, with directions to watch the motions of Mahboob, and if possible get hold of his guns.

In the beginning of June, the Colonel learnt that Mahboob's whole force, consisting of seven battalions of Nejeebs, with nineteen pieces of cannon, were within a few miles of him. He therefore marched towards them that night, and at day-break the next morning, saw them drawn up in front of him, about a mile in distance; their guns in the centre, with four battalions on the right, and three on the left of the park; their line bending in, so as nearly to form a half-moon. The Colonel immediately put his two battalions in order, and marched forward in a column by subdivisions from the right. Mahboob was not present; but the next in command, not suspecting the Colonel's intention to attack him, fired a salute of nineteen guns; which, however, Colonel Parker took no notice of, but marched on until he came within fifty or sixty paces of them, when he beat to arms, and the divisions doubled up on the left, and formed a line in front of them. The whole having been loaded as soon as they saw Mahboob's troops, were prepared for the meeting. The Colonel advanced into the centre, between the two lines, and called for the commanding officer, who moved forward to meet him, desiring to know his commands. The Colonel told him he must have his guns, which the other said he could not surrender without consulting the commander of the artillery, who being called for, declared, " that he had lived a man of honour for more than forty years, and that he would not now disgrace himself by giving up what had been entrusted to his charge." The Colonel gave him half an hour to consider it, and if they did not surrender them in that time, he would take them by force. He immediately pulled out his watch, which he held in his hand ; and both sides stood ready for the contest. At the expiration of the half hour, he very deliberately ordered his orderly drummer to beat the general, which was the signal to begin the action; when a salute of round and grape was thrown in, and the battalions gave their fire by subdivisions, with as much regularity as if it had been a field day. The Nejeebs were not idle: they returned a close fire, which did a good deal of execution; but before they had time to load again, the Colonel ordered the battalions to rush on the enemy with their bayonets, which decided the fate of the day, as they fled in every direction, leaving their guns behind them, which the Colonel* carried back in triumph to Korah; and this battalion has ever

* This gallant officer lost his life whilst serving with Goddard's detachment, in the retreat from the Maharatta country, on the 23d of April, 1781. He covered the rear of the army down the Ghauts, and being mounted on a white charger, became a mark for the enemy, one of whom shot him through the body.

since worn a cannon as a device on their turbans.

Lieutenant John Erskine, who acted as interpreter to Colonel Parker, was killed, and Captain Gravely had his leg broke, of which wound he died a few months after. The Colonel had then orders to return to Belgram.

During the war with the Maharattas and Hyder Ally, this battalion was not actively employed, nor was it any way engaged in service until after the second war with Tippoo in 1793, when it was sent to Assam, under Captain Thomas Welsh, against one of the chiefs of that country, who had raised disturbances on the frontier of Rungpore; and after that service was effected, it rejoined its brigade. In 1796, it became attached to this regiment.

The Twenty-fourth Battalion—which was included in the other two to complete this regiment, was raised at Cawnpore in the year 1778, by Captain Kilpatrick, whose name it bore whilst a battalion. In 1781, it was formed into a regiment, and ordered to the coast; where in every action it distinguished itself, much to the satisfaction of the late Sir Eyre Coote. In June, 1783, the twenty-fourth regiment, being then in the lines before Cuddalore, the French European regiments made a sally, when this corps nobly received them on the points of their bayonets, and repulsed them, at which time, Captain James Williamson, and Lieutenant Ochterlony,* were wounded at their head.

It returned to Bengal in January, 1785,

* Now Major-General Sir David Ochterlony, Baronet, and K. C. B. who has been recently distinguished in the Nepaul war of 1814 and 1815.

and has not, the writer thinks, been since on active service, until it joined the 7th Regiment.

EIGHTH REGIMENT

was composed of the 8th, 30th, and 33d battalions.

First Battalion.—This corps was raised at Bankypore in the year 1761, by Captain (late Lieutenant General) Giles Stibbert, and was intended for the duty of the Patna factory.

After the defeat of the Shah Zadah by Major Carnac, the beginning of 1761, the army returned to Patna, where Colonel Coote, who had just arrived from Madras, took the command of it; but he getting into a dispute with the Nabob Cossim

Ally, who was then with the army, regarding Rajah Ramnarain, the collector of Patna, the colonel was recalled in June that year, when Major Carnac again succeeded to the command. He was then directed to leave a detachment for the protection of Patna, and to return to Calcutta with the rest of the troops. He therefore ordered this battalion with two companies of Europeans, which he thought sufficient for that duty. However Mr. Macguire, then chief of Patna, differed with respect to the strength of the party, which he thought, at least, ought to be doubled. Both parties wrote to Calcutta, and the Board decided in favour of Mr. Macguire. In consequence of this the Major was desired to leave four companies of European infantry, with one company of artillery, and three battalions of Sepoys, which were those of Captains

Turner, Tabby, and Wilson, with a proper complement of guns.

As this was the unfortunate detachment on which that monster Cossim Ally wreaked his vengeance after he heard that the Council had restored Meer Jaffier to the musnud, it is to be hoped that an account of it will not be unacceptable, just as the writer had it from an intelligent serjeant, who fortunately escaped that inhuman massacre.

Shortly after Major Carnac left Patna with the rest of the army, Mr. Macguire quitted the chiefship, and Mr. Ellis was nominated in his room.

At the same time Captain Carstairs, one of the officers who had resigned in 1758, and had then returned from Europe, restored to the service, was appointed to the command of the detachment. In those days the civil servants had the sole controul of the military. They gave out the parole, and all orders from the Council passed through them.

Mr. Ellis appears to have been a man of a very warm temper, and had, unfortunately for himself and those under his command, conceived the greatest dislike to the Nabob Cossim Ally. The latter end of 1762, and a great part of the year 1763, was passed by the Board in negociating with the Nabob, and for the adjustment of some differences which had arisen between the agents of private gentlemen, and the officers of government, regarding trade.

At this time, although Patna was garrisoned by the troops of Cossim Ally, yet the hospital for the accommodation of the sick Europeans, was in the Chaleesssatoon, and Dr. Fullarton, who had charge of them, was allowed to reside in the city.

The European soldiers had also the privilege of visiting their sick friends, whenever they could procure a pass from their officers.

In this state of things, Mr. Ellis, from what motive is not known, came to the unaccountable resolution of attacking the city of Patna. On consulting with Captain Carstairs, it was determined to make the assault a little before day-break on the 6th of June, 1763. Accordingly, at three o'clock in the morning the detachment paraded at the house of Mr. Ellis, at Bankypore, and from thence they proceeded to Patna, accompanied by Mr. Ellis and all the civil servants then at the factory. The attack was made on the north-west angle, nearly opposite the old factory, where a few Europeans and Sepoys ascended the wall by ladders, and immediately pushed down, opened the sally-port, and admitted the rest of the detachment.

The killadar made scarcely any resistance, but with his garrison fled out of the east gate towards Futwa, so that by sunrise the troops were in quiet possession of the city. The necessary guards being placed, Mr. Ellis returned to Bankypore with all the gentlemen of the civil service, and Captain Carstairs, to breakfast; and it is supposed, that the few officers left with the men became negligent, not suspecting any danger, as the chief who ought to have been well-informed, had left them.

The killadar, hearing of the disorderly state in which the troops were, immediately assembled his garrison, carried the east gate with little resistance, and drove the troops before him like a flock of sheep; so that in the course of a few hours, he was once more placed in his command.

The flying detachment took shelter in the old Factory, where they were joined by Captain Carstairs and the gentlemen from Bankypore.

By this time the whole of the country about Patna were in arms, all complaining of the treacherous manner in which the city had been attacked by the English, and vowing vengeance against them. The killadar instantly sent an express to the Nabob, who was then at Monghyr, informing him of what had happened; which so exasperated Cossim Ally, that he dispatched an order to cut off Mr. Amyett, who had been deputed to him by the Council, and had left him only two days before. He was overtaken near Moorshedabad, and most cruelly put to death, with two other gentlemen who were with him.

The situation of Mr. Ellis, with all the detachment in the Factory, became alarming. They were surrounded by enemies, and had no hopes of succour from any quarter, as the navigation of the river was entirely in the hands of the Nabob as low as the river Hoogly. In the mean time the killadar had mounted guns on the bastion which commanded the Factory, and played upon them so smartly that it was dangerous to appear at any of the windows. However, a few light guns were hoisted up to the upper story, from which the fire was returned, but with little effect. In this state things remained for four days, when it was determined to cross the river, and by forced marches try to reach the dominions of Sujah Dowla, who being then on good terms with the Company, they were in hopes of obtaining his protection. Boats being collected, the whole crossed quietly in the night, and the next morning took up their line of march by the way of Choprah; but the whole country being against them, they found it difficult even to procure provisions. However they fought their way until they reached Manjee, where the troops of the Nabob surrounded them. The rains had before this set in with great violence, and almost the whole country was under water. They nevertheless drew up once more to face the enemy, although their ammunition was nearly expended. The Europeans upon a high spot in the centre, with Turner's battalion on the right, Tabby's on the left, and Wilson's in the rear. The enemy began the attack, but Turner's battalion advancing upon them with fixed bayonets drove them back; and had they been supported, it was thought the detachment might have extricated itself, and stood its ground for a day or two longer; but the Europeans, worn out with fatigue and want of nourishment, refused to charge, and in consequence the whole laid down their arms, and surrendered prisoners of war.

Thus was a body of nearly three thousand fine fellows lost to the service, and the Honourable Company involved in a war at a most unseasonable time, by the rashness and impolicy of one man.

The whole being sent to Patna, most of the Sepoys entered into the Nabob's service, and the remainder were dismissed. A number of the foreigners also took service with Cossim Ally, but the rest of the Europeans were kept in prison until the Nabob heard that the Board had reinstated Meer Jaffier on the musnud, and then he came to the resolution of putting them to death. It is said that some of his officers refused to execute those cruel orders, until Somroo, a foreigner, who had deserted from the Company's service, undertook the bloody deed.

All the gentlemen of the civil service, with the officers and men in confinement, were slaughtered; and it is reported that most of them sold their lives very dearly. Captain Carstairs* died, as was supposed, of a broken heart, before the prisoners reached Patna, and was buried at Hadjipore, where a monument is erected to his memory. Doctor Fullarton, who had some friends at Court, had his life spared; and four British serjeants escaped.

These men were selected from the other prisoners, and sent to the Nabob of Pur-

* He was an Ensign in 1756, and wounded in the defence of old Fort William, but got on board one of the ships in the river, and by that means escaped the Black Hole.

nea, (as he was then called,) and placed under his charge.

When Cossim Ally had determined upon the destruction of the prisoners, he sent orders to Purnea for these men to be put to death. The Nabob, who happened to be a humane, good man, and being highly pleased with the conduct of the serjeants whilst with him, declined putting the orders in execution. He, however, wrote to Cossim Ally, entreating that he would recal his mandate, because he feared, if he was still determined upon it, it would be a difficult matter (as the men were beloved by all his people) to find one that would undertake the task. Cossim Ally, on the receipt of the letter, flew into a violent rage, and directed another order to be sent to the Nabob, in which he told him, that if he had not spirit himself to put his commands in force against those faithless and treacherous Englishmen, to send them immediately to Patna, where ample justice should be done, for the crimes they had committed.

On this letter being delivered to the Nabob, he sent for the serjeants, and with tears in his eyes, informed them of the severe order he had received, and of the steps he had taken to preserve their lives; that he must now send them to Patna, where he hoped by the time they got there, the rage of Cossim Ally might be cooled, and that they might probably escape death. They were accordingly embarked on a Pattella boat, in charge of a jemadar and twelve burkendosses, and dropped down a small stream called the old, or little Coosy, which falls into the Ganges a little below Bissunpore Gola, and nearly opposite to Sickra Gully.

Here the serjeants had determined to

K

have a chance for their lives. As soon as the boat had reached the Ganges, and hoisted sails for Patna, it being the height of the rains, two of them went up on the chopper, or roof, and saw the jemadar and three or four of his men asleep, with their faces covered. This they thought a favourable opportunity. They gently seized two of their swords which were near them, drew them from the scabbards, and having at the same time secured the matchlocks, one of them ran up to the Manjee, (helmsman,) seized him by the arm, and threw him overboard: they then gave a hurra, which was the signal for the two below; who, in the meantime, were not idle. The noise waked those upon deck, who seeing the serjeants with drawn swords, fell upon their knees, and begged their lives, which were granted, provided no further resistance was made. The je-

madar instantly called to his men below to
surrender, which they did; so that the
serjeants were in possession of the boat in
less than ten minutes from their first going
upon deck. The Manjee having caught
hold of the rudder, entreated to be taken
on board, and promised that he would
conduct them down the river. His request was complied with, and the moment
he was placed in his former situation, the
sails were hauled down, the boat put
about, and the crew taking to the oars,
the gallant fellows had the good fortune,
by sunset, to meet the British army under
Major Adams, then advanced to Udda
Nulla.*

* As all these deserving men have long since paid the
debt of nature, the writer entreats he may be excused in
giving a short account of them. Their names were Davis, Douglas, Speedy, and another whose name he cannot
now recollect. Davis was a smart young man, and a native
of Edinburgh. He enlisted in the Company's service in

K 2

But to return to Captain Stibbert's battalion.

On the army reaching Calcutta in 1762,

the year 1761 and was posted to Captain Sommors's company, one of those left at Patna, in which he was soon made a serjeant. After his escape from Purnea, he was put into the grenadiers, with which he served the whole war. Being posted to the 1st brigade, that division of the army proceeded to Monghyr, where, in the year 1766, the general resignation took place. In this situation of things, Sir Robert Fletcher, who commanded the brigade, sent for Davis and offered him a commission; but he nobly refused it, declaring, " that as the officers could not live upon their pay, which was the cause of their quitting the service, it was impossible he could." He was, however, the next year appointed Quarter-Master to the three battalions sent to the coast under Lieutenant Colonel William Smith, and on the return of that detachment in the year 1770, procured an ensign's commission, and died a captain in February, 1788.

Douglas was a brave soldier, and was long in the service of the Honourable Company in Bengal. On his joining the army at Udda Nulla, he was placed in the European battalion, with which he served until the year 1766, when he was appointed serjeant-major to one of the Purgunnah battalions, then formed for the Revenue duty at Moradbaug.

Here he remained until the beginning of the year 1773, when the Sanassies becoming very troublesome in the dis-

a detachment of two battalions of Sepoys,
of which this was one, and two companies

trict of Rungpore, Captain Timothy Edwards, who then
commanded the battalion, was ordered out with five companies, to clear the province of those marauders. Having
received his instructions from the Chief of Rungpore, he
marched in quest of them, and the morning after, having
crossed one of those small rivers with which the northern
districts abound, he descried the Sanassies about two miles in
front of him. He immediately formed his detachment into
a column by subdivisions from the right, and marched on
towards the enemy, who, as soon as he came near enough,
saluted him with a few rockets. When Captain Edwards
thought himself within a proper distance for engaging, he
rode to the head of the column, and beat to arms, intend-
ing that the divisions should double upon the left of the
leading division as they came up; but the men mistaking
the orders, wheeled to the left, and formed in battalion,
which laid their right flank open to the enemy. Seeing
the error they had fallen into, he galloped to the left, in
order to draw them into line fronting the Sanassies, whilst
Douglas exerted himself on the right for the same purpose;
but it was too late, for the enemy, perceiving the confusion,
rushed in upon them with their swords and spears, and
having dispatched a few, put the rest to flight.

Douglas was one of the first that fell; but the fate of
Captain Edwards was not known: his hat was found in
the Nulla before-mentioned, but the body has never been
discovered.

K 3

of Europeans, were sent to Jellasore, under the command of Major Knox, where

The Native Commandant and Adjutant were tried for their misconduct in that unfortunate action, and were executed at the mouth of a cannon: but the gallant behaviour of one of the jemadars deserves much praise; for having rallied sixteen men, he made his retreat good, although attacked on every side by the Sanassies; for which he was promoted to the rank of a Subadar.

This was the third detachment which had been cut off by those religious plunderers; one commanded by a Captain Thomas, the other by Lieutenant Keith, who both lost their lives upon the occasion. As these parties were all from the Purgunnah Battalions, it occasioned the dissolution of that establishment.

Serjeant Speedy, from whom the writer had the account of Captain Carstairs's detachment, was a steady soldier, and a man of long service in the field. He was a native of Ireland, and in the beginning of what is called the Spanish or ten years war, enlisted in the 32d regiment of foot, then commanded by Colonel Huske. He accompanied his regiment to Flanders in the year 1742, and remained with it the whole war; was present at the battles of Dettingen, Fontenay and Lafeldt; in the latter of which he lost two fingers of his left hand. The following year, being 1748, he received his discharge, and immediately after enlisted in the Honourable East India Company's service. He arrived at Madras in 1749, and being posted to the grenadier company, was ordered to take the field

they remained until July, 1763, when they
were ordered to join the army under

under Major Lawrence, where he served the whole of the
war against the French, in which many gallant actions were
performed by the company he belonged to. In 1756 his
Company composed part of the detachment sent round to
Bengal, under Major Kilpatrick. And here the writer
begs leave to observe, that the Company above mentioned
was the foundation of the grenadier company of the only
European regiment belonging to our Honourable employers
now in Bengal, and it affords him the highest gratification
to learn, that on a late occasion,* the officers and men
composing it, nobly supported the character which it had
acquired by their gallant predecessors fifty years before.

From the time of his arrival in Bengal, until he was
posted to Captain Turner's battalion, in the year 1760, he
was present in every action which occurred during that
period. On his return from Purnea, he was posted to
the European regiment, in which he died in the year
1767.

The other Serjeant was a man of great merit for his situation in life. Shortly after he joined the army from
Purnea, he was appointed Serjeant Major to Captain
Scotland's battalion, then ordered to be raised at Midnapore, where he died in 1765.

* At the battle of Deeg, in November, 1804, and subsequent service during the late Maharatta war, the Ho-

Major Adams; since which time this bat-
tálion has gone by the name of the Jellasore. It continued with the army the
whole war; and had a share in every action which took place during the contest.
In April, 1764, Captain Stibbert being
the oldest in the service, this battalion
became the First in number.

At the battle of Buxar it was posted on
the right of the front line; and when
Major Munro ordered it to advance to attack in flank a battery, as has been already
mentioned, Lieutenant James Nicol (late
Lieutenant General) being a lieutenant in
the battalion, but acting Adjutant to the
Sepoy corps, (and as such rode in the
suite of the Commander in Chief,) imme-

nourable Company's Bengal European regiment eminently
supported its character for gallantry and discipline; and
sustained very serious loss, both in officers and men.

diately dismounted, and gallantly led his battalion forward : but he was driven back with considerable loss, and the corps thrown into great confusion : however he soon rallied his men, and kept up with the front until the enemy were defeated.

On the formation of the brigades it was posted to the Second, and repaired with the other corps to Allahabad, where it remained until the latter end of the year 1766, when it was relieved by the third brigade. It was not afterwards employed, until 1774, when it was one of the battalions engaged with the Rohillas in the battle of St. George, where it acquitted itself as usual.

In 1775, when General Clavering's regulations took place, it became the Eighth in number, which rank it still retains.

In 1796, it became the 1st battalion of this regiment.

Second Battalion.—This corps was raised at Chunar, by Captain William Davies, in 1779, and it still bears his name.

The writer does not recollect of its ever being actively employed, previous to 1796.

The Thirty-third Battalion—which was divided between the other two, was one of the Charrie Yaries formed from the old corps in 1786.

———————

NINTH REGIMENT

was formed from the 9th, 29th, and 84th Battalions.

First Battalion.—This corps was raised

at Burdwan, about the year 1760, and still retains the name of that province; but being the second battalion which had been formed there, it is called the " Choota, or Second, Burdwan."

In 1763, it was commanded by Captain William Smith, and according to his rank, became the Eighth in number. It was actively employed during the whole of the severe campaign under Major Adams, as it was the following year under Majors Carnac and Munro, and was one of the eight battalions at the battle of Buxar, where its conduct, as upon every other occasion, was highly meritorious.

In 1765, it was posted to the Second Brigade, and remained at Allahabad until the following year, when it was relieved by the Third Brigade; after which it had no opportunity of distinguishing itself until 1774, when it formed part of the army which attacked and defeated the Rohilla chiefs at the battle of St. George. It was then commanded by Captain Thomas Smith. The next year it became the Ninth in number, in consequence of General Clavering's regulations.

This arrangement might, at that time, appear very pretty upon paper; but it certainly caused a good deal of uneasiness, and some little confusion in the army, from which it did not recover for two or three years. In the British army, when troops are brigaded, old and young corps are mixed together; but here the rule was departed from, and all the old battalions of the Second and Third Brigades thrown into the back-ground, and deprived of their rank in the line, merely for the sake of seeing the numbers in regular succession on the general return. -Every corps in these two brigades lost their standing; for although the 21st, the youngest battalion in the Third Brigade, did not change its number, yet it was superseded by the 24th battalion, which was taken from the Purgunnah establishment, and placed in the line as number Fourteen.

From that time, the writer does not recollect any particular service that this battalion has been upon, until it came into this regiment in 1796.

Second Battalion.—This is one of the battalions formed in Oude, by British officers, for the service of the Vizier, in 1776. In 1777, it was commanded by Captain Thomas Naylor, whose name it now bears.

It was this corps that disarmed and dispersed the 15th battalion, when it mutinied at Midnapore in the year 1795.

Captain John Bradley had then the command of it. The following year it came into this regiment.

The Thirty-fourth—which completed the two before-mentioned battalions, was one of the Charrie Yaries, formed from old corps in 1786.

TENTH REGIMENT

was formed from the 10th, 14th, and 18th, battalions; all old corps.

First Battalion,—This battalion was raised at Midnapore, the beginning of 1764, by Captain Scotland, whose name it still bears. It was then the Sixteenth in number. The following year it was posted to the Second Brigade, and was ordered to Allahabad.

In 1772, it was commanded by Captain Richard Ewens, and in November that year was ordered to join Captain Camac, in the Ramgur district. The day after its arrival at Ramgur, Captain Camac, being the senior officer, ordered this battalion to be under arms in the afternoon, that he might look at it. Accordingly at four o'clock, all the officers having dined with him, they repaired to the parade, where the battalion was drawn up.

The officers having taken post, Captain Ewens began the exercise, and had got about the middle of the Manual, which in those days was performed six deep, when a Sepoy was observed to quit the ranks; but it was supposed to be upon some occasion of no consequence. The exercise went on, and at the conclusion of the

Manual, the rear half-files having doubled up, the battalion was just going to prepare for the charge, when the Sepoy who had been in the rear was perceived coming round the right flank, with recovered arms; but as it was imagined he was not well, and wished for his Captain's permission to quit the field, no notice was taken of him. He therefore walked on until he came within two yards of Captain Ewens, when he levelled his piece and shot him through the body.

On Captain Ewens falling, the battalion instantly broke, and rushed forward to revenge his death; but Captain Camac, with great presence of mind, ordered them to return to their ranks, and that ample justice should be done. He immediately sent one of his officers to bring down his own battalion, (the 24th,) and on its arrival he ordered a drum-head General Court-

Martial to try the murderer, who sentenced him to be drawn asunder by tattoos. The horses being fastened to his limbs, many attempts were made to draw them from the body, but without effect; and then the Sepoys were allowed to put him to death, which they did with their swords. Captain Ewens only lived a few hours. His brother, Lieutenant Ewens, was at his post in front of the battalion, and saw him fall; and it is supposed that the shock occasioned the insanity which shortly after afflicted him. He died a few years ago in Calcutta, then under the care of Doctor Dick.

It seems that the fellow who committed the murder had been a havaldar, or serjeant, and in consequence of some misconduct during the march from Dinapore, had been tried by a Court-Martial, and reduced to the ranks; which it is supposed induced him to take revenge on his Captain. The writer has not been able to learn of what cast he was.

Captain Akerman succeeded to the command of the battalion, and in 1774, marched with it into Rohilcund, where it was present at the battle of St. George. The following year it became the Tenth in number, in consequence of General Clavering's arrangement.

In 1794, it was again in Rohilcund; and on the 26th October, when the action with the Rohillas took place, it was the flank battalion of the left wing, and as such was ordered out of the line to protect the baggage. It was then commanded by Captain William Mackintosh.

In 1796, it formed a part of this regiment.

Second Battalion.—This corps was raised

at Allahabad, by General Smith, in order to complete the Second Brigade, in 1765; and having been formed in the Mahometan month of Mohorum, it was denominated the " Hooseney Battalion," which appel-lation it still retains. It was then num-bered the Twentieth.

In 1774, it served the whole campaign in Rohilcund, and was present at the battle of St. George, where its behaviour was steady and soldier-like. The following year, on General Clavering's plan being put in force, it became the Thirteenth in number, which in 1783 was altered to the Fourteenth. During the war with the Maharattas and Hyder Ally, it was not out of the Company's provinces; but in the year 1790, was ordered to the coast, then commanded by Captain Archdeacon, who lost his life at the head of it, 6th February, 1792, under Lord Cornwallis, when he attacked the lines of Tippoo Sultan, near the walls of Seringapatam. Lieutenant Henry White, (now Major-General Sir H. White, K. C. B.) being the senior officer, immediately took the command, and moved forward to the support of the Commander in Chief, then in a very critical situation: for which good conduct he was allowed to continue in command of the corps until its return to Bengal in 1793, when Captain Hyndman, who had commanded one of the Volunteer battalions on the same service, was placed at the head of it; and the following year accompanied the army to Rohilcund, where, in the action which took place on the 26th October, its steadiness was remarkable; for on the removal of the 10th battalion to take charge of the baggage, it became the flank corps, and formed an angle for the protection of that wing. The Rohillas made many attempts to break in upon them, but the battalion preserved its countenance so well, that they could not succeed. Two years after it came into this regiment.

The Eighteenth Battalion completed this regiment.

It was an old and distinguished corps, and it is to be lamented that it was not placed in a situation where it could have preserved its name. It was raised at Patna, the latter end of 1763, by Captain James Morgan, whose name it bore as long as it existed as a battalion, and was the Eleventh in number. It was employed on active service almost immediately. In April, 1764, it joined the army under Major Carnac before Patna, and took its post in the line of entrenchment with the old corps. The same year it accompanied the army to Buxàr, where, on its arrival the morning of the 22d October, it was placed in a village about a thousand yards in front of the encampment, to watch the motions of the enemy; where it remained until the commencement of the action the following day, when it was ordered into the line; but not however until it had lost upwards of one hundred men. Its captain, (the late colonel,) James Morgan, was at the head of it the whole day, although far from being in a good state of health. Its lieutenant was the late Colonel Knudson, and its ensign the late Major General Erskine.

In 1765, it joined the third brigade at Bankypore, and a noble battalion it appeared to be. In those days, before the brigades were formed, the captains commanding battalions regulated the uniform and dress of their men. Some corps were faced with blue, some yellow, &c. according to the fancy of the commander; but when once fixed could not be altered without permission from the Honourable Board. When the brigades were formed, Lord Clive fixed the uniforms himself, which were the three dark colours, viz. the first blue, the second black, and the third green. The latter, however, was changed to yellow in 1779, at the request of Colonel Ironside.

When the Morgan battalion was formed, it had white facings, white turbans with red ends, and white cumberbands with a red cross; and its colours were the flag of St. George. In 1775, by General Clavering's regulations, it became the Seventeenth in number, which was changed to the Eighteenth in 1783.

After it had joined the brigade, it was

not actively employed for some years. In 1786, Major Bolton got the command of it, and from that time it was considered as the finest battalion in the service. In 1794, it accompanied the army into Rohilcund, and was pitched upon by Sir Robert Abercrombie to form a part of the reserve with the European battalion and the thirteenth of Sepoys; which was posted on the right of the line in the battle which was fought on the 26th of October. The misbehaviour of the cavalry that day threw those fine corps into confusion; and the enemy's horse and foot getting in among them at the same time, a dreadful slaughter was the consequence.

Major Bolton was unfortunately killed, but he sold his life nobly; for being a powerful man, he cut down four of the enemy with his own hand; but in making a stroke at a fifth, his sword broke in the hilt, and he was then cut to pieces.*

In 1796, this fine battalion was incorporated with the two before-mentioned, although originally senior to them both.

ELEVENTH REGIMENT

was formed from the 11th, 19th, and 26th Battalion.

First Battalion—was raised at Mooshedabad in the year 1764, by the late Co-

---

* This battalion under Major Bolton's command was considered the highest disciplined corps in the service; and in the action in which it lost its commander it had nearly 200 men killed and wounded. Such was their steadiness under arms, that it was observed, the killed and wounded were lying in their ranks as regular as when drawn up on parade. For an account of that battle, see Appendix.

lonel Dow, (then a captain,) and it bears his name to this day. It was then the Eighteenth in number; and as soon as it was formed was ordered to the army, and joined it at Benares about a month after the battle of Buxar.

In 1765, it formed part of the second brigade, and was stationed at Allahabad, until relieved the following year, by the third brigade.

In 1774, it marched into Rohilcund, and was present at the battle of St. George, fought on the 23d April that year. Since which the writer does not recollect any active service it has been upon. In 1775, it became the twelfth in number, but on the reduction of the Mathews battalion in 1783, it changed to the Eleventh.

In 1796 it formed part of this regiment.

Second Battalion.—This corps was raised at Bankypore in 1765, by Colonel Sir Robert Barker, in order to complete his brigade, and it still goes by his name.

In 1766 it accompanied the brigade to Allahabad, and the following year Sir Robert Barker fearing that the Fort would be unhealthy for the Europeans, during the warm months, sent the regiment to a mango grove about two miles on the other side of the Jumna, where temporary barracks were built for them; and this battalion was ordered to accompany the regiment.*

* This season was the most unhealthy for Europeans ever remembered; and it extended to every part of the country. Even at Monghyr, which is considered equal in salubrity to any part of India, the first European regiment lost a number of officers and men. But at Allahabad the mortality was great. In the single month of June, the 3d regiment lost seven officers and nearly forty privates, most of them the stoutest men in the corps. The artillery company lost one officer and four or five men. The officers who died were Captains Fielding and Nu-

In 1769, the brigade moved down from
Allahabad to Dinapore cantonments, then
just finished for the reception of troops ;
and two years after was ordered to the
Presidency. In March, 1773, the third

gent; Captain Lieutenant Black of the artillery; Lieutenant Roberts, Ensigns Cleland, Morrison, Kitchen and
Buchanan. The last five died in one day, being the 10th
of June. The principal cause of it shall be briefly related.

The troops had been out that morning to attend an execution. Eight men had deserted from the regiment, and
when taken were tried, and all sentenced to die. Two of
them being English were to be shot, and the six foreigners
to be hanged. General Smith, the commander in chief,
then at Allahabad, pardoned six of them, but they were to
take it by lot of a single die, and it fell on two foreigners,
who were immediately executed. Before it was over, it
was past nine o'clock, and the sun powerful to a degree.

Lieutenant Roberts, on returning to his tent, feeling
himself excessively warm, ordered a few pots of cold water to be thrown over him, which checked perspiration,
and brought on a high fever that terminated his existence
in less than an hour. On the report of Mr. Knight, the
Surgeon Major, that the body would not keep, Colonel
Grant, who then commanded the regiment, ordered it to
be interred immediately; and it being Ensign Cleland's
tour of duty, he was directed to attend. On his return,

brigade, which was in a high state of discipline, exhibited a grand spectacle on
the race-course of Calcutta.   It was a
review of the Third European regiment
then consisting of two battalions, of about
four hundred and fifty men each, and two
battalions of Sepoys, viz. the twelfth and
this battalion, with sixteen field-pieces.
The infantry fired twenty-six rounds per
man, in every situation which in those
days it was thought proper to form troops
into; and notwithstanding the extent of

he was himself taken ill, and before two o'clock was a
corpse. Ensign Morrison, who was upon the most intimate terms with Mr. Cleland, not having heard of his
death, ran into his tent to speak to him, and seeing his
friend dead, fell down in a fit. He was, however, recovered, and taken to his tent, where he begged to be removed to the Fort. His request was complied with, and
Ensigns Kitchen and Buchanan, who were his shipmates,
accompanied him in the cool of the evening, but they all
three died in the course of the night.

Two European ladies also died about the same time—
a Mrs. Nugent and a Miss Allen.

line, not a single mistake happened the whole day. Colonel Hugh Grant commanded the troops; Mr. Hastings and Sir Robert Barker being in front. The artillery fired quick, as if in action, during the whole of the manœuvres, and it had a fine effect.

In the latter end of the year, this battalion, with the rest of the brigade, marched up to Berhampore, and two years after to the field station, where it remained until November, 1777, when it was once more ordered to the Presidency. In March, 1778, Colonel Ironside having then the command of the brigade, presented Mr. Hastings with another review, but it was on a smaller scale—only the 3d regiment, which at that time was (as indeed it always had been) in a high state of discipline, and four companies of grenadier Sepoys, two of them from this battalion, and two from the Duffield, with four guns. The regiment went through the Manual, firings, and manœuvres by itself, and when it came to what was supposed to be the concluding volley and charge, the Europeans and Sepoys broke, and ran towards the Fort, but in less than a minute the drums beat to arms, and the adjutant having previously placed the two stands of colours at about two hundred yards distance from, and facing each other; the troops immediately formed upon them, with a company of Sepoy Grenadiers on each flank. The sham fight then began, each division of the regiment firing by sub and grand-divisions as they advanced, until they came within fifty yards of each other; when the whole fired a volley by word of command from the Colonel, which was so close that it might be taken for a single cannon. The

lines then charged in quick time; and
when the bayonets came to lock, the
whole recovered their arms; by signal
turned to the right, and wheeled by files
from the right of each subdivision to the
front, passing through each other, until
they had got to the same distance as
before, when they formed in line facing
each other. The attack began a second
time, and ended in the same manner,
highly to the satisfaction of the Governor
General, and of General Stibbert, who
accompanied him to the field.

This battalion has always been considered as a fine corps, although it had seen
very little, if any, active service, until it
became incorporated in this regiment.
When General Clavering's regulations
were carried into execution, this was the
only battalion which retained its original
number. Afterwards, by the reduction

of the Mathews, and the old 19th, which was broke at Midnapore, it became the Nineteenth, by which number it came into this regiment.

The Twenty-sixth Battalion—which was divided between the other two, was a corps that had seen a good deal of service. It was raised at Cawnpore in 1778, by Captain John Byrne, whose name it bore as long as it was a separate battalion; although it was sometimes called " the Dobie-ka-Pulton," Captain Byrne having enlisted a number of washermen from the adjacent villages

In 1781, it was formed into a regiment of two battalions, and ordered to the coast, where it served the whole war with much credit. It returned to Bengal the latter end of 1784, then commanded by Captain Richard Scott, where it remained

M

until the breaking out of the war with Tippoo Sahib in the year 1790, when it was again sent to the coast, still commanded by Captain Richard Scott, and served, as before, with high reputation.

In 1796, it was incorporated in this regiment.

TWELFTH REGIMENT

was composed of the 12th, 17th, and 21st battalions.

First Battalion.—This corps has been long distinguished for its steadiness and gallantry in the field; and it affords the writer the highest satisfaction to learn, that it fully supported that character during the late arduous contest,* the particulars of which will, of course, be given by a more able hand, in due time.

It was raised at Monghyr, the latter end of the year 1763, by Captain (late Colonel) John White, whose name it still bears, and became the Twelfth in number, the rank which it now holds, although once changed.

As soon as it was formed, it was ordered to the field, and joined the army near Benares.

In 1765, it was posted to the Third Brigade, in which it became a favourite corps; although every battalion composing it were in such high order, and so correct in all their manœuvres, that the writer has no hesitation in saying, that from that brigade, which was long and

* The Maharatta war of 1803, 1804, and 1805.

ably commanded by Colonel Gilbert Ironside, the Bengal Infantry had the ground-work of their discipline.

It continued some years with its brigade without an opportunity of distinguishing itself, except on parade duty. It was one of the battalions reviewed in Calcutta, 1773.

In 1775, by the arrangement of General Clavering, it became the Eighteenth in number; and in the beginning of 1781, it was formed into a regiment, with its old number, and was ordered to the coast under that excellent officer the late Lieutenant-Colonel Edmonstone, then a Major, where its conduct during those severe campaigns against Hyder Ally, and his son Tippoo Sahib, was highly spoken of. On the conclusion of the war, it returned to Bengal, but did not reach Ghyretty until the beginning of 1785, where the Governor-General, Mr. Hastings, met and complimented them on their meritorious services, and return to their families and friends.

In 1794, it was again ordered to the field, under Sir Robert Abercrombie, against the Rohilla chiefs, and was present in the action of the 26th of October, commanded by Captain Edwards, but being in the centre, had little opportunity of shewing itself to any particular advantage, except by its steady countenance. Two years after it was formed into this regiment.

Second Battalion.—This is the oldest corps in Bengal, but by a strange turn of fortune, became the last battalion in the whole service, when incorporated in this regiment.

It was raised at Calcutta, in January.

M 3

1757, and being the first corps that had ever been regularly clothed, it long went by the appellation of " Laul-Pulton," or Red Battalion ; although latterly it has been generally known by the name of " Galliez," the cause of which will be mentioned hereafter.

Before it was quite disciplined, it was ordered to accompany the army under Colonel Clive, first to the attack of Chandernagore, and then to the battle of Plassey, fought on the 23d of June, where it acquitted itself as well as could be expected for so young a corps. In 1758, it accompanied Colonel Ford to the Northern Sircars, where it distinguished itself in a particular manner, with its old friend the Mathews. In 1759, or 1760, it was again in motion under the same officer, against the Dutch, in which it assisted in defeating and taking prisoners nearly the whole of them. It afterwards served under Colonel Cailland, and was one of the corps present at the dethroning of the Nabob Meer Jaffier, and the placing of his son-in-law, Cossim Ally, on the Musnud. In short, wherever service offered, the Laul-Pulton and the Mathews were, in those days, sure to be called upon.

In the beginning of 1761, it served under Major Carnac in the attack and defeat of the Shah Zadah, after which it returned to Patna with the army, where it remained until 1762, when it was ordered to the Presidency. In 1763, on the war breaking out with Cossim Ally, it was early in the field, and served with distinguished bravery during the whole contest.

In November that year, Captain (now Colonel) Primrose Galliez got the command of it. At Sant, during the mutiny in February, 1764, it shewed some symptoms of insubordination, but they were prevented from rising to any height at that time, by the interference of their officers. It accompanied Major Carnac to Patna, where, in the attack of the lines by Sujah Dowlah, on the 3d of May, it acquitted itself with its usual gallantry.

On the retreat of the combined army from before Patna, this battalion, with the Marines and European Grenadiers, and the battalions of Mathews and Trevanion, were ordered to scour the Choprah district, which they completely did as far as Sewan; and on their return from thence, this battalion, with the Marines, were ordered to halt at Manjie. About a month after, the Marines were ordered into Choprah; and now, the battalion being left to itself, the seeds of disaffection, which were sown at Sant about seven months before, began to ripen, and in a short time broke out into open mutiny; the men declaring they would serve no longer, as the promises made them had not been fulfilled. At first they imprisoned their officers, but released them from confinement the following day, and allowed them to return to Choprah. As soon as information of the mutiny had reached Choprah, the Marines and Captain Trevanion's battalion were ordered out at an hour's warning, in pursuit of them, as has been already mentioned. In four days they returned to Choprah with the whole of the mutineers, where they were met by Major Munro, who had just taken the command of the army, and had come over from Choprah to see the detachment.

Hearing of what had passed at Sant, and the misbehaviour of this battalion upon the present occasion, he thought it right to make a severe example; and a severe, although necessary, example it undoubtedly was. He ordered eight-and-twenty of the most culpable to be picked out, and tried by a drum-head general court-martial, when the whole were sentenced to suffer death. The eight guns, with the detachment, being brought out, the first eight were fixed to their muzzles and blown away. Here it was, that three of the grenadiers entreated to be fastened to the guns on the right, declaring, that as they always fought on the right, they hoped their last request would be complied with, by being suffered to die in the post of honour. Their petition was granted, and they were the first executed. I am sure there was not a dry eye amongst the Marines who witnessed this execution, although they had long been accustomed to hard service; and two of them had actually been on the execution party which

Grenadier Sepoy.

Published by J. Murray, Albemarle Street ...

shot Admiral Byng, in the year 1757. The other twenty were ordered to the several stations of the army, where they all suffered death in the same manner. After which, the battalion was weeded of such men as had been active in the mutiny, and then ordered to Patna, where it was again completed; since which it has generally gone by the name of its Captain, " Galliez." A little before this, it was fixed as the Ninth in number, being the rank of its commander. It remained at Patna until after the battle of Buxar, when it again joined the army.

In 1765, it was posted to the Third Brigade. Its uniform was then blue facings, blue turbans and cumberbands, and made a handsome appearance under arms. It remained many years with its brigade, before it had an opportunity of distinguishing itself again. In 1775, on the regulations of General Clavering taking place, it became the Sixteenth in number, which was afterwards, in 1783, changed to the Seventeenth. In 1776, it accompanied the brigade to Belgram, from whence it was shortly afterwards detached, with its old friend the Trevanion, (now called the Duffield,) under the command of the late Colonel Parker, as has been already noticed; and in the action at Korah, which took place the beginning of June, it was posted on the left, then commanded by Captain (now Lieutenant-General) William Jones, where it gallantly bore the fire of four battalions of Neejeebs, drawn up on the right of their guns. However, a timely charge of the bayonet dispersed that immense body. Lieutenant Erskine, who fell in the action, belonged to this battalion.

It returned to the Presidency in 1778,

after which the writer does not recollect its being on any service until 1796, when it came into this regiment.*

The Twenty-first Battalion—which, with the other two, completed this regiment, was one of the corps formed for the service of the Vizier by British officers, and afterwards taken into the Company's service. It was first commanded by Captain (now Lieutenant-General) Stuart, whose name it bore as long as it was a separate battalion. This battalion was in the action of the 26th October, 1794, in Rohilcund, and sustained some loss. It was then commanded by Captain Knowles.

---

* Since finishing the foregoing, the writer has heard of the gallant conduct of this excellent corps, during the late Maharatta war, the particulars of which, he trusts, will soon be given to the public. July, 1807.

Thus far has the writer, to the best of his abilities, fulfilled the task which he undertook. He fears there may be some mistakes, but can assure his readers that they are not intentional; and he has no doubt, should these few sheets fall into the hands of any of the old officers, who were sharers in the scenes he has described, but they will do him the justice to say, that he has not misrepresented them.

He found some trouble in separating the old from the new corps, as the frequent alterations which had taken place during the last forty years made it difficult to distinguish one from the other; but particularly the regulation of 1775, which destroyed the regular rank of the whole Native army.

When the foregoing establishment of twelve regiments was formed by the regulations of 1796, the incorporation of bat-

talions into regiments was necessarily
governed by the local situation of corps
at the time; yet it must ever be regretted,
that they should have been so unfortunately stationed, as to occasion such an
old and fine corps as the 18th, or Morgan's
Battalion, to lose its name and consequence as a distinct body; whilst the
29th, 30th, and 31st, preserved their Hindoostanee appellation and rank in the line
by becoming Second Battalions.

The same remark is applicable to the
late 24th and 26th Battalions, those corps
having been highly distinguished on foreign service; especially the 24th, which
acquired immortal honour before Cuddalore, in the year 1783.

AN ABSTRACT

Of the Active Service on which the several Battalions have been employed.

Regiment.	Battalions.	Hindoostanee Names.	Plassey, battle, 1757.	Buxar, battle, 1764.	On the Coast, 1767.	Battle of St. George, in Rohilcund, 1774.	Battle of Korah, 1776.	Bombay, 1778.	Coast, 1781.	Coast, 1790.	Rohilcund, battle, 1794.
1st	1st	Burdwan		1				1			1
	13th	Blane							1	1	1
	32d	Charri Yarie									1
2d	2d	Grant		1	1			1			
	25th	Bowles							1		
	28th	Landeg								1	
3d	3d	Gowen			1					1	
	22d	Young									
	27th	Kallie									
4th	4th	Burra, (or 1st) Crawford						1			
	31st	Chutta, (or 2d) Crawford									
	37th										
5th	5th	Ironside				1		1			
	23d	Baillie									
	35th	Charri Yarie									
6th	6th	Swinton		1	1			1			1
	20th	Raje									1
	36th	Charri Yarie									
7th	7th	Goddard						1		1	
	16th	Duffield		1			1				
	24th	Kilpatrick							1		
8th	8th	Jellasore		1		1					
	30th	Davis									
	33d	Charri Yarie									
9th	9th	Burdwan, (2d)		1		1					
	29th	Naylor									
	34th	Charri Yarie									
10th	10th	Scotland				1					1
	14th	Howseney				1				1	1
	18th	Morgan		1							
11th	11th	Dow				1					
	19th	Barker									
	26th	Byrne, (or Dobie) . . .							1	1	
12th	12th	White							1		1
	17th	Galliez, or Laul-Pulton	1				1				1
	21st	Stuart									1
		Total . . .	1	7	3	6	2	6	5	6	10

SUPPLEMENT.

——————

The preceding Narrative having briefly described the foundation, services, and occasional modifications of the Sepoy corps in the service of the Honourable the East India Company, under the Presidency of Bengal, from the year 1756-7 down to the establishment of twelve regiments, as fixed by the regulations of 1796, by which the organization of corps, in regard to the number and rank of the European officers, and the general principles of arrangement and command were proposed to be more immediately assimilated to the system of European armies—it may be useful, previous to entering on a

continuation of the Narrative, in regard
to the subsequent formation and services
of corps respectively, down to the present
time, to take a short retrospect of the
general features and circumstances of the
service under its successive arrangements,
during the above period, together with
such incidental notice of relative occurrences connected with the subject, as
may have escaped the recollection, or not
fallen within the knowledge of the previous narrator.

By a list of the European officers of the
Bengal army in the year 1760, it appears
the number was as follows:

> Captains 19
> Lieutenants . . . 26
> Ensigns 15
> Total 60

For the List of Names; and also a Memorandum of the strength of the Bengal army in 1756, see Appendix A.

By the preceding account we find that 1764. in 1764, there were nineteen battalions of Sepoys in the service, which were severally commanded and paid by officers of the rank of captain, with a small portion of European subaltern officers and serjeants under them. In October of that year the battle of Buxar was fought with much professional skill, judgment, and courage; and the complement of European officers to Native corps at that time, appears to have been one captain, one lieutenant, and one ensign to each battalion.

Three Bengal Sepoy battalions were 1767-8-9. detached on service into the Northern Circars, under the command of Lieutenant-Colonel Wm. Smith, on whose death

Lieutenant-Colonel Peach, who came into the army in 1764, as a major, from His Majesty's service, was appointed to command the Bengal troops on service in the Circars, the object of which was to assist the Presidency of Fort St. George, at that time engaged in war with Hyder Ally and his French allies.

In 1769, those troops were recalled to Bengal, when a part, or the whole, embarked to return by sea. On which occasion, the flank, or two grenadier companies, of the 3d, or Gowen's battalion, perished by shipwreck, the ship on which they embarked having never been heard of afterwards. This unfortunate occurrence made a fatal impression on the minds of the Native troops, with regard to sea voyages, which, joined to their previous religious and habitual prejudices, required the lapse of many years, and much conciliatory management to overcome.

The establishment of Sepoy battalions 1774-5. was increased to twenty-one, and formed into three brigades.

On St. George's day, 1774, the Rohillah battle was fought on the plains of Rohilkund, in which six Sepoy battalions were engaged, together with the 2d European regiment under the command of Colonel Champion, then the Commander in Chief, in Bengal. They were opposed to a superior number of a very brave and hardy race of men—devoted to their leader, whose cause was their own, fighting for the country and home which he had established for them, in the fruitful province of Khuttair. Their gallant chief fell early in the action, when the discipline and valour of the British troops, and the execution of their artillery, soon spread terror and dismay among the Rohillah bands, and led to a prompt and decided victory.

1775-6.   Lieutenant-General Sir John Clavering succeeded to the office of Commander in Chief towards the close of 1774, and after having reviewed many of the Sepoy battalions, His Excellency was pleased to record his sentiments by the expression of admiration and wonder at the state of discipline to which the Sepoy corps had been brought, declaring that he found them in no respect inferior to any regiment in His Majesty's service.

1777-8.   Nine battalions were added to the establishment by the transfer to the Honourable Company's army of that number of corps which had been disciplined by British officers for the service of His Excellency the Newaub Vizier.

At the beginning of this year the Presidency of Bombay having been seriously embarrassed by the pressure of the Maharatta war, which then prevailed, the Governor General was convinced of the necessity for effectual succour, both in specie and troops, being afforded to that quarter of the Honourable Company's possessions, with as little delay as possible. Supplies of the former had been, and could again be, sent by sea, in the course of six weeks, or two months voyage, (as well as by bills through the medium of the native bankers of Benares,) but no such resource presented itself with regard to troops.

On this emergency the comprehensive mind of Warren Hastings formed the resolution (on his own responsibility, it was understood, when opposed by a majority of his colleagues in the government) to

order a compact yet efficient detachment
of Native troops from the Bengal army,
to march across the continent of India,
" through hostile and unknown regions,
from the banks of the Ganges to the
western coast of India"—with the view,
in the first place, of creating a diversion
in the councils and operations of the
enemy, and eventually co-operating with
the Bombay government and forces in
the prosecution of the war in which they
were engaged.

A force was accordingly ordered to as-
semble at Cawnpore, composed of the
following details, under the command of
Lieut. Colonel M. Leslie.

Six battalions of Sepoys, viz. the
    1st, 2d, 4th, 5th, 6th, and 7th,
    900 rank and file each   . . 5,400
One regiment of Native cavalry   600

One company of Gholundauz,
    or Native artillery   100
Candahar horse   500
    Total fighting men 6,600

With 103 European officers.

The followers of this detachment were composed as follows :

Servants and followers . . . 19,000

Bazar Department.—A complete
    establishment of which was dis-
    tinctly attached to each corps,
    without any expense to govern-
    ment, and to the essential aid
    thereby afforded, in the ready
    supply of provisions, &c. may
    be mainly ascribed the success-
    ful progress of the detach-
    ment 12,000

Total followers and bazar people 31,000

The body of Candahar horse were in

the service of the Newaub Vizier, and
were ordered by His Excellency to accompany the detachment, as a proof of
the interest he felt for the prosperity of
the Honourable Company's government.
These were a very brave and hardy race
of Mussulmen, natives of Candahar and
Cabool, were very well mounted, commanded by a respectable chief of their
own clan, and highly distinguished themselves by their fidelity and valour throughout the long and arduous service in which
the detachment was engaged.

The pressing necessity for the intended
aid superseded every consideration of con-
venience, and therefore as soon as the
whole were in readiness to move, the detachment commenced its march, and
passed the river Jumna at Calpee on the
12th of June, 1778; at the hottest time of
the year, with the still more inclement

season of the periodical rains close at
hand. For a striking illustration of the
character of the Native troops on that
occasion, see Appendix B.

The severity of the season, and the assumed necessity of conciliating the different chieftains of the countries through
which the detachment had to pass,* occasioned a long halt at Chatterpoore, and
afterwards at Rajegurh in the province
of Bundelkund; and Lieutenant-Colonel
Leslie, who commanded the detachment,
died at the latter place on the 3d of October.

Lieut. Colonel Tho. Goddard succeeded

* Perhaps an unauthorized interference with their political relations—at which delay the Governor General was
extremely disappointed and displeased; and an order was
on the way to camp for Colonel Goddard to supersede
Colonel Leslie in the command of the detachment at the
time of Colonel Leslie's death.

Colonel Leslie in the command, and on the 8th of October, the detachment prosecuted its march under the direction of that able and distinguished officer.

On the 30th of November they reached the banks of the river Nerbudda, and there halted in the vicinity of Husseinabad, waiting communication with the government of Bombay, until the 16th of January, 1779, when they again resumed their march, and arrived at Surat on the confines of the Gulf of Cambay on the 25th of February, 1779.

After a very short interval of repose, this gallant band took the field against the enemy, and nobly distinguished itself through a series of seve reand arduous service, down to the close of the general war in Europe, and in Asia in 1783.

Colonel Goddard was advanced to the rank of Brigadier-General for the eminent zeal and ability which he displayed in his situation of command throughout the war; at the close of which he embarked for Europe for the recovery of his health, but died just as the ship reached the Land's End of England. The name and memory of Goddard will be yet long cherished with admiration by the European officers, and the Native soldiery of the Honourable Company's army.

The remains of this meritorious detachment returned nearly by the same route that it went across the continent of India, and reached the frontier provinces under the Presidency of Bengal, at the close of the year 1784, under the command of Colonel (now Lieutenant-General) Charles Morgan; reduced by the casualties of the service on which it had been employed to less than one half of the original complement of the corps. Honorary standards were granted to each of the battalions—gold medals to the Subadars, silver medals to the Jemadars, and likewise to every non-warrant officer and private Sepoy who served with the detachment from the commencement of the expedition until its return into the provinces.

As a further mark of the approbation of Government, an additional pay of one rupee per month was granted to each non-warrant officer and Sepoy, who had served during the whole period above-mentioned. For the testimony recorded by Government, in regard to the important services of this detachment, see Appendix C.

1778-9. In consequence of the general war in Europe and in Asia, nine more Sepoy Battalions were raised, making a total of thirty-three battalions, besides three Independent, or Local Corps; and exclusive of the six battalions then serving in the west of India, under General Goddard.

Early in 1779, Lieutenant-General Sir Eyre Coote succeeded to the office of Commander in Chief. On the augmentation of the army, the troops were disposed into four brigades, with a Colonel at the head of each, viz. : The three brigades as before, with a proportion of the increase added to each ; and the Independent Brigade, which was still paid by the Vizier, and was stationed accordingly for the more immediate duties and protection of his Excellency's dominions.

During the years 1779 and 1780, the Commander in Chief reviewed every corps in the army, and his report and opinion on that occasion reflected the highest honour on the Native Corps, and their European officers. His Excellency more particularly distinguished the corps in

Oude, although the most remote from the superintendence and controul of superior authority, as " some of the finest corps he had ever seen in the field."

In the month of August, 1780, a detachment of about 2,000 Sepoys, under the command of Major (now Lieutenant-General) William Popham, captured by escalade the important and, till then, deemed impregnable fortress of Gwallior,* after having previously carried the fort of Lahore by assault, and compelled an army of 15,000 Maharattas to evacuate the districts of Gohud and Gwallior.

1780-1.   Five battalions of Sepoys, with artillery, and some regiments of cavalry, under Lieutenant-Colonel Camac, were employ-

* The success of this bold enterprize was materially promoted by the whole of the troops employed on the escalade having been provided with shoes made of strong cloth, quilted with cotton, for the occasion.

ed in the province of Malwa, against Madajee Scendiah, one of the most powerful chiefs of the Maharatta confederacy. That little army was frequently surrounded by large bodies of Maharatta horse, and suffered great privation and hardship, both from being greatly in arrears of pay, and much straitened for provisions. Their situation at one time became so extremely critical, that a large reinforcement was ordered to hasten to their support, under Colonel Muir. Meantime, before that succour arrived, Lieutenant-Colonel Camac resolved to make a forced march, and attack the camp of Madajee Scendiah, in which he completely succeeded, taking all the enemy's guns, camp equipage, and elephants, with a large and very welcome supply of grain.

This brilliant exploit may be considered 1781. as an important crisis of the war; for in

o

the month of October, 1781, Colonel Muir, (who, being the senior officer, had, on joining, taken the command of all the troops on that service,) acting under instructions from Mr. Hastings, the Governor-General, concluded a separate treaty with Madajee Scendiah, which was speedily followed by a general peace with all the Maharatta States.

From 1764, down to the close of the year 1780, the Sepoy corps appear to have continued on the same footing, in regard to internal economy and arrangement; with occasional fluctuations in the strength of the corps, and the number of European officers.

In January, 1781, a new formation, combined with a considerable augmentation of the Native army, and an increase of European officers, was carried into effect.

Thirty-six regiments were then formed,

(exclusive of the six battalions serving in 1781, the west of India,) consisting of two battalions each, and each battalion of five companies of 100 rank and file each. A Major-Commandant was placed at the head of each regiment; a Captain to command each battalion; with a Lieutenant to each company.

An European Adjutant was appointed to each regiment, in the person of one of the Lieutenants, as non-effective Staff; and a Native warrant-officer was appointed Adjutant to each battalion. Two European non-commissioned officers were likewise appointed to each battalion, as Serjeant-Major and Quarter-Master Serjeant.

The appointment of Native Commandant, which had hitherto existed in each battalion on the old establishment, was abolished.

The pay of each battalion was drawn

1781. in one abstract by the Captain, and it was ordered to be issued to the men in the presence of the Lieutenants commanding companies; for the due performance of which they were declared responsible, and were required to make a report and declaration, on honour, in writing, that the men had been duly paid.

That emolument may have been sometimes derived from the payment of the men, when vested in the uncontrouled management of the officer at the head of the corps, cannot perhaps be denied; but there seems to have been something very objectionable in the system now adopted, which placed the subaltern officers in the awkward predicament of superintending the conduct of their commanding officer; and reversing the principle of check or controul, was liable either to be rendered nugatory, or be productive of jealousy, litigation, or discord.

The defeat of Colonel Baillie's detach- 1781.
ment in the Carnatic, by Hyder Ally,
towards the close of the preceding year,
and the pressure of the war in that quarter, rendered recourse to Bengal for succour, in money, provisions, and troops,
urgently necessary; and happily for the
interests of the Honourable Company, and
the reputation of our arms, the wisdom
and decision of the Governor-General were
equal to every emergency.

The new formation of the Bengal Sepoy
corps was no sooner carried into effect,
early in 1781, than Mr. Hastings resolved
on sending five regiments to the relief of
the Presidency of Fort St. George. This
force was accordingly assembled at Mednapoor, and consisted of the following
regiments, under the command of Colonel
Thomas Deane Pearse, of the Bengal
Artillery, who was selected by the Gover-

1781. nor-General to command the detachment. The regiments were,—the 12th, commanded by Major Edmonstone; the 13th, by Major Blane; the 24th, by Major Kilpatrick; the 25th, by Major Wedderburne; and the 26th, by Major Byrne.

In the meantime the Commander-in-Chief, Sir Eyre Coote, had embarked with such European troops as could be spared from Bengal, and proceeded to the Carnatic, to conduct the war in person.

On the occasion of corps assembling at Mednapoor for the intended service, one regiment, the 19th, proved to be in a state of insubordination, owing to some prize-money claims not having been duly adjusted by its commanding officer, for which he was dismissed the service, by the sentence of a Court-Martial, and the regiment was broken, and drafted into the other corps proceeding on foreign service.

The detachment proceeded on its march 1781. through Orissa and the Northern Circars, and having reached the vicinity of Madras about the middle of the year 1781, the Bengal troops joined the other forces in the field, under their distinguished Commander-in-Chief, the late General Sir Eyre Coote; and during the arduous warfare in which they were engaged from that period, down to the cessation of hostilities before Cuddalore, in June, 1783, the Bengal corps, collectively and individually, established for themselves and the army to which they belonged, a proud and lasting reputation. The veteran remains of those gallant corps returned to Bengal, early in the year 1785, when their encampment was visited by the Governor-General in person, and the grateful testimony which he recorded on that occasion is no less creditable to the generous feel-

1781. ings of his own mind, than it is decisive of the high military character and virtues of the Native soldiery of Bengal. For copy of which see Appendix D.

In the autumn of this year, the revolt of Rajah Cheyt Sing, and the consequent insurrection in the province of Benares and the adjacent countries, occurred; when not only the military character, but the fidelity and attachment of the Native soldiery was put to the severest test, and redounded highly to their honour.

A large portion of the army having been at that time on foreign service in the west of India, in the Carnatic, and in Malwa, the number of troops applicable to Home Service was very limited, and the corps were widely dispersed; so that not only was the person of the Governor-General, Warren Hastings, in imminent danger, but the very existence of our

speedy reduction of the hill-fortress of 1781. Bidzygurh, and the other strong-holds possessed by the Rajah, to the westward of the Ganges.

Previous to quitting this portion of the narrative, it will not be deemed an unsuitable digression to quote a paragraph or two from Mr. Hastings's statement of that period, for which see Appendix E.

About the close of this year, Government 1782. ment ordered the 4th, 15th, and 17th regiments, which were at Barrackpoor, and the 35th which was at one of the stations higher up the country, to be held in readiness for foreign service. This force, it was understood, was intended to proceed to the Northern Circars, or to Hydrabad, under the command of Lieutenant-Colonel Popham.*　But a rumour

---

* The object was probably to take possession of the Guntoor Circar, which about that time devolved to the Honourable Company consequent to a former treaty.

1782. was spread amongst the troops, that it was meant for them to proceed by sea; to which measure, such was still the insuperable aversion of the Native soldiery, that the regiments above-mentioned which were at Barrackpoor, entered into a general combination not to proceed on the service for which they were ordered; and on two or three companies being ordered from one of those corps to precede the march of the detachment, for the purpose of taking charge of stores and provisions, the three regiments made known their determined resolution that those companies should not be allowed to march; and as there was only one other regiment at the station, Government had no present means of enforcing obedience to its orders.

The foregoing was however the only act of positive disobedience or mutiny that the men were guilty of—no violence, nor other disorderly conduct was committed;

they continued to treat their officers with the usual respect, and the duties of the corps were carried on as usual; notwithstanding that some Native officers and men who had been the ringleaders in the combinations, were confined in the quarter-guards of their respective regiments; nor was any attempt made to release them.

After the lapse of several weeks a General Court-Martial was held, when two Subadars of the 15th, and one or two Sepoys, were sentenced to suffer death, by being blown away from the mouths of cannon. The sentence was carried into execution, in the presence of those regiments which had mutinied, and one other regiment only, which happened to be at the station, without any other symptoms but those of pity for the fate of their misguided leaders. The 35th regiment

1782. likewise mutinied on its march towards
the appointed rendezvous. The four regiments were afterwards publicly pardoned in General Orders. But on the
return of the six battalions from the west
of India in 1784, those four regiments
were broken, and the officers and men
were drafted into the six battalions, on
their being formed into regiments, an arrangement which had been deferred until
their return from foreign service.

Such was the occasion, on which the
original Mathews's battalion (then the
4th regiment) was doomed to end its
career, after having been for a long course
of years, as stated in the preceding Narrative, one of the most distinguished and
meritorious corps in the service.

1785. Early in 1785, in consequence of the
general peace in Europe and in Asia, and
of the return to Bengal of the " two Great

Detachments" from the Carnatic, and the west of India, the Native infantry establishment was reduced to 30 regiments, after incorporating in that number, the six old battalions returned from Bombay. All the corps in excess to thirty were disbanded. The Native warrant and non-warrant officers were retained on their pay as supernumeraries, to fill vacancies as they occurred in the several Native corps of the army, and the privates had the option, to the extent of the numbers required, to be enrolled on the strength of corps returned from foreign service. By those measures, a large portion of European as well as Native officers became supernumerary; and a total stagnation of promotion, in both branches of the service, was the consequence for several succeeding years.

Early in 1786, at which time Lieutenant-

1786. General Sir Robert Sloper was Commander in Chief, the Sepoy corps were again new modelled, in consequence perhaps of the Honourable the Court of Directors having expressed their disapprobation of the regimental system which took place in 1781. In regard to which they observed, that they saw no good reason for placing a Major at the head of each regiment, when the duty could have been performed by a Captain, nor for appointing a Captain to the command of each battalion, when the situation might have been very well filled by a Lieutenant.

The 30 regiments were now formed into 30 separate battalions of 10 companies each, under the command of a Captain, or a supernumerary Major on Captain's allowances; to whose hands the payment of the corps, and all its interior authority and management again reverted.

European subaltern officers were con- tinued in the proportion of one for each company.

General Orders dated in March of this year directed that the Native officers of the Sepoy corps should thenceforward be denominated commissioned and non-commissioned officers, instead of warrant and non-warrant; and to the former, throughout the army, commissions were accordingly issued under the signature of the Commander in Chief; in lieu of the warrants which in time past had been granted by the Colonels commanding brigades.

In the course of this year, detailed orders for a peace establishment for the several Presidencies in India were received from the Court of Directors, which caused another revision of the Native Infantry establishment of Bengal.

Thirty-six battalions were now formed,

P

1786. consisting of eight companies only each, and each company only 68 privates.

Five of the six additional battalions were formed by the transfer of companies from the old corps, and the new ones were, by the Natives, generally denominated Chari Yarie battalions, meaning " The Four Friends," in allusion to their having been severally composed of details from four corps. The Ramgurh Provincial Corps was brought into the line as the 31st battalion.

Captains were directed by the Court's orders to command the Sepoy battalions, as had been previously arranged by the Local Government; and the 36 battalions were divided into six brigades, with a Lieutenant-Colonel and a Major at the head of each brigade. The complement of European subaltern officers of one for each company was continued; a Serjeant for each company was likewise specified 1786. in the Honourable Court's orders; but this was not carried into effect. Three European non-commissioned officers were allotted to each battalion, as Serjeant Major, Quarter-Master Serjeant, and Drill Serjeant; but the latter was again struck off by the orders of government in 1788.

Supernumerary Majors were still considered eligible to the command of battalions on Captains' allowances; and supernumerary Captains were posted in the proportion of one to each battalion, on the allowances of Lieutenant; but were ordered always to proceed in command of every detachment or division of two or more companies, or even a less force.

In the month of September this year, the Right Honourable Earl Cornwallis entered on the office of Commander in

1786.   Chief, as well as that of Governor-General of India.

1787.   In the course of the year 1787, the Commander in Chief made a tour of the provinces, and visited all the military stations of the army. His Lordship viewed with no less admiration than astonishment, the very high military condition and proficiency of the Native corps of the Bengal army.

After having seen all the troops at the field-stations, Lord Cornwallis caused a memorandum to be circulated, in which his Lordship noticed some points of minutiæ in regard to the exercise and field-movements of corps, which he wished should be uniformly observed by all; and at the same time expressed the " greatest satisfaction at the appearance and good order of the troops, which had convinced him of the zeal and attention of the officers of the Bengal army." Applause from such an exalted character was well calculated to cherish the spirit of professional pride and emulation, which was otherwise liable to be much depressed at that time, owing to the great reductions which had taken place, thereby creating long lists of supernumerary officers of all ranks, and causing a general stagnation of promotion.

The sole authority, together with the payment of the corps, having reverted to the Captains commanding battalions, by the regulations now in force since 1786, they were in many instances very tenacious of that authority; whilst the aspiring subalterns were restless, and disheartened at being precluded from a proper degree of intercourse, authority, and consideration, with the companies to which they were yet nominally attached. This state of things naturally produced instances of

1787. litigation, jealousy, and discord; and in consequence of some representations made to the Commander in Chief, his Lordship, under a strong impression of the necessity for supporting authority, issued an order in the course of this year, directing, that as the appointment of subalterns to particular companies had given rise to difference of opinion, on the nature of the duty in that rank, it was in future left to the discretion of officers commanding Native battalions, to employ the subaltern officers in the manner that they might think would best promote the good of the service.

This latitude was not, in every instance, exercised with becoming moderation; and in the year 1790, his Lordship found it necessary by a further order, to observe, that understanding that in consequence of the discretion granted to commanding officers of battalions of Sepoys, in 1787, it was the practice in some battalions to leave the European subaltern officers entirely unposted to companies; it was therefore now directed, that each subaltern officer in a battalion should be attached to distinct companies; leaving it to commanding officers to post the subaltern officers to companies, in such manner as they might deem proper, as well as to prescribe the regimental duties required of them as officers attached to companies.

A short acquaintance with the Bengal army satisfied the discerning mind of Earl Cornwallis, that the Native soldiery possessed every requisite quality of good and efficient troops, with the exception of one particular, which was yet a desideratum, to overcome their aversion to sea-voyages, in order to extend their services to other Presidencies and parts of India,

1789. with the promptitude and facility which was attainable by sea, instead of the protracted period necessarily occupied in marching by land, as exemplified during the late war, in the instance of the " two Great Detachments," which marched to the relief of the Presidencies of Fort St. George and Bombay.

His Lordship was therefore determined to make an experiment for the gradual introduction and accomplishment of this important object, for which an opportunity presented itself early in this year.

In the month of January, dispatches were received from Bencoolen, apprising the Bengal Government that serious incursions had been made on some of the East India Company's settlements on the north-west coast of Sumatra, and representing the urgent necessity for a reinforcement of troops from Bengal. Lord

Cornwallis immediately signified his wish 1789.
that the three battalions of the 4th brigade,
then at the Presidency, viz. the 1st, the
30th, and the 32d, should furnish four
companies of Volunteers for that service;
at the same time promising a bounty of
ten rupees per man, to such as should
turn out.

After the first surprize occasioned by
this novel call had somewhat subsided,
the exhortations of the commanding, and
the other European officers, began to prevail; and in the course of three or four
days, a large portion of the requisite number of volunteers turned out from the three
battalions.

Daily reports of the progress of the
measure were made to head-quarters, and
it was the painful duty of the commanding
officer of the 32d battalion to acquaint his
Lordship, that two Subadars of that corps

1789. Suffice it to say, that by the happy union of example and encouragement, the detachment was speedily completed by volunteers, when they were formed into four companies, and six European officers were appointed: one to command the detachment, viz. Lieutenant (now Major-General) M'Cullock; one as Adjutant; and one to the command of each of the companies.

A regular Indiaman was ordered for the conveyance of the troops to Sumatra, with the most rigid instructions to the Commander, to render the situation of the Sepoys as comfortable as possible whilst on board; and to prevent any conduct of an offensive nature whatsoever on the part of the seamen towards the troops during the voyage.

The Sepoys superintended the filling of their water, the casks of which were all

carefully marked ; and they were required
to state every sort of article they wished
for, for their diet during the voyage, of
which an ample supply was provided accordingly, at the expense of Government.

Although the ten rupees bounty was
promised to be paid on their embarkation,
Lord Cornwallis acceded to the request
of the officers for its being paid before
they embarked ; and this confidence was
well requited by the men, the whole
having remained steady to their purpose,
and embarked without a single desertion.

They sailed the end of February, and
reached Sumatra in about five weeks,
without a single casualty or accident.
They remained there till the end of October, and suffered much from sickness.

The moment Lord Cornwallis received
accounts that the services of the detachment were no longer required at Sumatra,

expedition has occupied a larger space
than the circumstances of it might seem
to require, in this place: but it is, in fact,
to be considered as forming a very important epoch in the history of the Native
soldiery of Bengal. Since, however it
may have been swallowed up or forgotten
in the lapse of time, it is unquestionably
to be viewed as the origin of the cheerful
facility with which the Native troops
have, on many successive occasions, volunteered their services beyond sea, as
soon as the wishes of Government have
been made known to them; and the measures which were adopted on that occasion
constituted the basis of the rules and regulations which have since been invariably
adopted on every embarkation of Native
troops.

It is therefore to the spirit of conciliation and discernment which was evinced

served with distinguished reputation and applause throughout the war, and after its conclusion the detachment was ordered to canton in the Carnatic, at Saloor Pætt, between the Pullicat Hills, and lake of the same name, where it remained during the months of June, July, August, and September, 1792; awaiting the best season for their return-march to Bengal.

Towards the close of the year 1790, Earl Cornwallis resolved to proceed to the coast for the purpose of conducting the war in person. And his Lordship embraced the occasion for following up the experiment which had succeeded so well the preceding year, of inducing the Native troops to proceed on foreign service by sea. The wishes of government were accordingly communicated to a few of the battalions which happened to be the nearest to the Presidency, that two battalions

1790. of volunteers were required to be formed for service in Mysore, and to proceed to Madras by sea, with the Commander in Chief.

More than the number required soon turned out, and the battalions were speedily formed, and embarked under the command of Captain Thomas Welsh and Captain Henry Hyndman, who were selected by the Commander in Chief to command the volunteer battalions.

They partook of all the service which occurred under his Lordship's personal command during the war, and cantoned at the close of it with their comrades, the other six battalions at Saloor Pætt.

1791. On the close of the campaign, by the retreat from Seringapatnam about the middle of this year, dispatches were received in Bengal, communicating a call for 900 volunteer Sepoys to fill up the eight battalions serving in Mysore. On 1791. this being notified to the nine battalions nearest at hand, such was the spirit of emulation among them, that more than the number required soon turned out, and were speedily collected at Calcutta, whence they embarked with a large portion of volunteer European officers, on board three Indiamen, and reached Madras in the course of eight or ten days; they thence joined the army in Mysore, and were divided among the eight battalions previous to the opening of the campaign towards the close of 1791.

During this war in Mysore, the Bengal battalions were allowed camp-equipage in the proportion of one large tent for each company, the Madras corps having been previously furnished with tents on that scale; though, as yet, no camp-equipage, except a bell-tent for the arms of each

1791. company, had ever been allowed to the Native troops on the Bengal establishment.

1792-3. The end of September, 1792, the Bengal detachment commenced its return-march from the Carnatic, under the command of Lieutenant-Colonel Cockerell, and after a very pleasant march, chiefly along the sea-coast, arrived, the end of January, 1793, on the banks of the Sooban Reeka, where the detachment was dissolved. The whole of the volunteers which composed the two battalions, as well as the supply of 1791, returned to their former corps; and the several battalions proceeded to the stations of their respective brigades in Bengal, Bahar, and Oude, comprising a progressive march of from 1500 to 2000 miles from the cantonment in the Carnatic to the frontier stations in Oude.

·Honorary standards were granted to the 1792-3, six battalions, and medals were conferred on all the Native officers and troops who had served in Mysore. For Lord Cornwallis's and Lt. Colonel Cockerell's thanks to the detachment, see Appendix F.

Leave of absence was granted to all the volunteers returned from foreign service on more favourable terms than usual, according to the example adopted in the instance of the Bencoolen Volunteers.

In 1792-3, a detachment of 15 companies of Native infantry was sent on service into the distant provinces of Assam, under the command of Captain Thomas Welsh.

Marquis Cornwallis returned to Bengal in August, 1792; and in August, 1793, his Lordship again embarked for the coast, in consequence of the war with France, and after the fall of Pondicherry,

1792-3. his Lordship embarked for England, and was succeeded in the command of the Bengal army by Lieutenant-General Sir Robert Abercromby, K. B. in the month of October, 1793.

1794.   In the year 1794, whilst the Commander in Chief was making a tour of inspection, a violent revolution took place in the hitherto happy state of Rampoor in Rohilkund, which had been governed with paternal solicitude by the Newaub Fyzoolah Khan, since the fall of Hafiz Rahmut, in the year 1774. The recent death of Fyzoolah Khan led to sanguinary feuds and irregular accession to the government, among his children; for the suppression of which the aid of the British troops was required by the Lord Paramount of the country, the Newaub Vizier.

The Commander in Chief took the field at the head of a large force, consisting of ten or eleven battalions of Native infantry, besides the 2d European regiment, two small regiments of cavalry, and an adequate complement of artillery.

On the 26th of October, 1794, the combatants came in sight of each other near the village of Bætoorah, on the plains of Rohilkund, not far from the scene of the former Rohilla battle, on St. George's day, 1774. The enemy pressed forward to offer battle; and in consequence of the great extent of ground covered by them, the Commander in Chief ordered the reserve, consisting of the 2d European regiment, with two choice battalions of Sepoys, viz. the 13th on the right, and the 18th on the left, to be brought into the line, of which those corps became the right wing; and the cavalry were also brought into line, forming on the right of the whole.

Upon those chosen corps composing the reserve, the enemy directed their principal attack, and were fast closing with them,

1794. when, by a lamentable fatality, which to this day has never been distinctly accounted for or understood, the officer commanding the cavalry gave the word of command for them to *wheel inwards* by quarter ranks, or such at least was the movement that took place; the consequence was, that they broke in headlong upon the 13th battalion, the ranks of which became disordered before the order of their gallant leader, Captain Norman M'Leod, to fire upon the cavalry, could be executed: the enemy, for whom nothing could possibly have been more favourable, rushed in sword in hand, and in many instances seized and turned aside the bayonets of our troops with one hand, whilst they made use of their broad swords with the other; and following up the impression thus made, they penetrated in like manner the ranks of the 2d European regiment, and the 18th Battalion,

killing and wounding a great number of 1794.
gallant officers and men of those three
corps.*   Many particulars of that action
having been accurately stated in the account of particular corps, in the preceding
part of this Narrative, more need not now
be added, beyond the statement of the
action which was published at the time;
and which will be found in the Appendix G.

Discipline and united effort having at
length overcome the display of as much
individual bravery and prowess as was
perhaps ever witnessed ; the enemy retired, and were pursued, till a convention
was agreed on with the principal chiefs
and relatives of the family—Gholam
Mahomed, who had assumed the govern-

* The officer who commanded the cavalry absconded
to avoid being brought to trial, which explains the foregoing remark, " that the cause of the fatal movement of
the cavalry in the battle of Bætoorah has never been properly accounted for.."

1794. ment, after murdering his elder brother, having fled his country, and has since remained an outlaw. The war being thus ended, the troops returned to cantonments.

1795. In the course of this year, government resolved on sending to Malacca a force equal to a battalion of Sepoys; and whether induced by the facility with which volunteers to proceed by sea had offered during the Mysore war, or to avoid what may have been viewed as involving some additional expense, trouble, and arrangement in drawing volunteers from different corps; it was resolved to make the experiment of sending a battalion collectively on that service.

The 15th Battalion, commanded by Captain Ludovick Grant, was a corps of very high character, and being near at hand, the proposition was made to it through its commanding officer to volunteer its services on a voyage to Malacca.

The advances of a commanding officer 1795. to men under his command, (and in the present instance under a rigorous system of discipline surpassing most other corps in the service,) in which doubtless his own feelings were strenuously engaged for the distinction which the object in view would confer on himself and his corps, could not easily be resisted by many among the Native officers and men, who may indeed have been ready and willing to undertake the voyage; whilst the remainder, under the influence of persuasion, subordination, and diffidence, did not venture to express their dissent.

The corps was soon reported to government as being willing to embark, but when the time arrived, a spirit of aversion shewed itself, which ended in a most determined mutiny, and the corps was declared by government to have been broken

1795. with infamy, and its colours burnt, after having been dispersed by another battalion, the Twenty-ninth, with field-pieces, to which the ill-fated Fifteenth had for a moment the temerity to oppose itself, under arms.

The conduct of the 29th Battalion, commanded by Captain Bradley, was applauded by government, as it justly deserved, for the steady fidelity and firmness which it evinced on this trying occasion.

It is doubtless to be regretted that the experiment was tried; the minds of the Native soldiery at large were not yet sufficiently matured and reconciled to the evils, with which they had been habitually accustomed to view sea-voyages; and thus a fine battalion was annihilated, and a stigma cast on the service. The very number Fifteen was desecrated and ordered to be left blank in the enumeration of Native corps.

In the course of this year government 1795.
resolved that a Native corps, to be denominated the Marine Battalion, should be
raised for the duties of the islands, viz.
Sumatra, Penang, &c.

This corps was ordered to consist of
twelve companies of 100 privates each,
to be commanded by a Captain, with
seven Lieutenants to command the detached portions of the corps. But the
European officers were borrowed from
the corps of the line, from which they
were to be occasionally relieved, and rejoin their corps.

Such a corps was highly necessary, and
soon became essentially useful and efficient. The island duties had hitherto
been performed in a desultory manner,
and the men, such as they were, remained
for years in their situations, contracting
most other habits but those of soldiers.

1795. In the same year government likewise resolved to re-establish a local corps for the duties of the Ramgurh frontier, whence the former corps of that description had been withdrawn into the line, during the reductions and changes of the year 1786.

The Ramgurh Battalion was orderedto be raised on the same establishment and strength as the battalions of the line, as far as regarded the Native part; to be commanded by a· Captain with a few European subaltern officers to do duty with it, from the regulars, as in the case of the Marine Battalion.

This has since proved a highly serviceable and meritorious corps, and has been augmented, as will be noticed hereafter.

In this year likewise, a corps of Native Militia was ordered to be raised for the judicial and commercial duties of Cal-

241

cutta and the adjccent districts. It was 1795.
placed in the first instance under the Town
Major, and consisted of eight companies
of ninety privates. It has subsequently
been augmented to sixteen or more companies of one hundred privates each, and
proves a very useful auxiliary body of
troops, by which the regulars are relieved
from a variety of irksome and harassing
duties.

It is now commanded by an officer of
any rank who may be favoured with the
patronage of the Governor-General, with
one other European officer, who performs
the duty of Adjutant to the corps.

We are now arrived at the year 1796, 1796.
which forms an important epoch in the
history of the East India Company's
army.

By the regulations then adopted, with
the view, among other points, of ameliora-

R

1796. tion and improvement in the situation of the European officers, that of giving to them an increased degree of promotion and rank, caused a total reformation of the Native corps, in regard to the system of authority, interior economy, and payment of the troops.

The whole Native Infantry Establishment was condensed into twelve unwieldy regiments, of two battalions each; each battalion consisting of ten companies, (two grenadier, and eight battalion companies,) and each company of two Native commissioned, ten non-commissioned officers, and eighty privates, as a peace establishment: and the complement of European officers was fixed at one colonel, two lieutenant-colonels, two majors, seven captains, one captain-lieutenant, twenty-two lieutenants, and ten ensigns, to each regiment. And thenceforward the principle of regimental rank and promotion (to the rank of Major, inclusive) was adopted 1796. throughout the Honourable Company's army.

The field officers, captains, and the requisite proportion of Lieutenants, were appointed to command the companies. The payment of the men was expressly confided to the officers commanding companies respectively, who were declared to be invested with the same authority as is exercised by captains in command of companies, in European corps.

Monthly muster rolls, and corresponding pay abstracts, were directed to be prepared by the officers commanding companies. A pay-hawuldar, corresponding to pay-serjeant, was allowed to each company ; and on every issue of pay, acquittance rolls, signed by every individual of each company, in testimony of having received his full and just demands, were

796. ordered to be delivered to the commanding officer of the battalion, by whom they
are laid before the commanding officer of
the regiment, and then lodged as records
in the regimental office.

The Staff appointment of Native Adjutant was abolished. An European Adjutant was appointed to each battalion,
and an Adjutant and Quarter-Master, in
one person, to each regiment.* All promotion of Native commissioned, and non-
commissioned officers, was ordered to be
published in regimental orders. The recommendation for non-commissioned, to
proceed from the officers commanding
companies ; and of commissioned officers,

* The appointment of Adjutant and Quarter-Master to
each regiment has been recently abolished, and in lieu
thereof, an additional staff officer has been appointed to
each battalion, under the denomination of Interpreter, who
is likewise to perform the duties of Quarter-Master.

from the officer commanding each bat- 1796.
talion.

. The enlisting of recruits was vested in
the officer commanding the battalion,
subject to the approval of the Colonel
Commandant, or officer commanding the
regiment, when present.

The men are enlisted under a declaration
to be explained to them at the time, for
three years; after which they may apply
for, and obtain their discharge, on two
months' notice, except in time of war; but
no bounty, nor other form of renewal takes
place, whatever may be the number of
years they may continue to serve : neither
is there any bounty, or other pecuniary
incitement, in the first instance.

. An oath of fidelity, obedience, &c. is
likewise directed to be administered to
each recruit, in front of the colours; (a very
salutary measure, which it is feared has

1796. fallen into disuse,) and certain articles of war are likewise ordered to be read and explained to the recruits at the same time.

When the regulations of 1781 were promulgated, it was then ordered, for the first time it is believed, that an abstract of the Articles of War relating to Mutiny and Desertion should be translated into Persian and Hindoostanee, and be read and explained once a month to the Native troops.

A revised and enlarged abstract and translation was now printed in the English, Persian, and Nagree characters, to which the form of the oath, and declaration abovementioned, was subjoined. Copies were sent to every corps, with orders that the Native officers and men should make themselves thoroughly acquainted with the rules and ordinances by which they are governed.

The power of granting leave of absence

was now likewise vested in commanding 1796. officers of regiments only, when present; in the case of battalions, or detachments separated from the Head-Quarters, the commanding officers of battalions and detachments have that power: in either case, the application and consequent selection of men for that indulgence, (which is one of very high gratification to the Native troops, to visit their families,) originates with the officers commanding companies.

It may be proper in this place, to say a few words on the system of jurisprudence by which the Native troops are governed.

The Native commissioned officers are tried by General Courts-Martial, composed of Native commissioned officers, at which interpreters are employed. The Court, interpreter, witnesses, and Judge Advocate, are all sworn, according to the forms of their respective religions:

1796. the proceedings are conducted and recorded by the Judge Advocate-General, or one of his Deputies, as usual at European General Courts-Martial.

Non-commissioned officers and privates are tried, for minor offences, by minor Courts-Martial; viz. regimental, battalion, detachment, &c. which are likewise composed of Native commissioned officers, with an European subaltern officer, denominated the Superintending Officer, for recording the proceedings.* At these also, the parties are now all sworn, since the same course was adopted for his Majesty's service.

General Courts-Martial were formerly held under the authority of Colonels com-

---

* In further perfection of this system, an interpreter, in the person of an European subaltern officer, has, since the year 1814, been established as a permanent staff with every Native corps in the service.

manding Brigades, but are now only held under the warrant and authority of the Commander in Chief.

Other Courts-Martial were held by authority of officers commanding corps, detachments, &c. and approved by the same authority; they possessed the power of dismissing, or inflicting corporal punishment, &c. over all non-commissioned officers and privates.

The regulations of 1796 directed, that at the head-quarters of each regiment, none other than Regimental Courts-Martial should be held, but in the case of battalions, or parts of battalions, being detached, Battalion and Detachment Courts-Martial are authorized. But by those regulations it was further directed, that neither commissioned, non-commissioned officers, nor privates, should be dismissed by the sentence of any other than

1796. a General Court-Martial. A power, however, was continued to commanding officers
of regiments to dismiss Sepoys who, from
misconduct or other cause, should be
deemed unfit for the service.

Perhaps it would have been better, that
the power of dismissing privates, at all
events, should still have been continued
to Regimental, Battalion, and Detachment Courts-Martial, instead of throwing
the odium of such measure on the commanding officer's personal exercise of
authority : besides, that courts-martial being precluded from that generally best and
most salutary course, are obliged to have
recourse to the alternative of corporal
punishment, the frequency of which is to
be deprecated with any troops, but especially so with reference to the mild, orderly,
and tractable conduct of the Native soldiery of Bengal.

The fitness, or suitability of the general 1796.
principles of military arrangement com-
prized in the regulations of 1796, will not
probably be questioned; but it is to be
observed, that the practical operation of
them is rendered nugatory in a very important point, by the operation of the col-
lateral rules of the service. Under the
previous system, all the officers who were
attached to corps were always present and
effective with them, (cases of sickness ex-
cepted,) but especially those in whose individual hands the powers of authority and
command were vested, and which was
accordingly not liable to fluctuation or
change. Whenever officers returned to
Europe, which, however, but seldom happened, they resigned the service, and all
officers employed as staff, and in every
situation whatsoever, out of the line of
their regimental duty, were invariably

1796. struck off the strength of corps, and their places were immediately supplied by others.

Under the present arrangement, the proportion of field officers and captains, being those in whom the exercise and responsibility of authority and controul are essentially reposed, is that of twelve to twenty companies: yet small as even this number is, were they actually retained for the duties of their corps, the theory and the practice would be somewhat assimilated; but the whole of the staff of the government, and of the army, inclusive of a heavy commissariat, with the numerous officers on furlough in Europe, and those employed with local corps, and in all other situations whatsoever, are borne on the strength, as component parts of companies and corps,— so the result is, that a very small portion of field officers and captains remains for the

duties of the corps ;* companies are conse- 1796.
quently, for the most part, in the charge
of subalterns, temporarily, and changing,
according to their occasional standing,
under the course of events; and thus
often devolving to the hands of very
young officers, whose professional, nor local
acquirements, may not have at all qua-
lified them for such a situation of authority, over men to whose character, language, and habits, they are yet more or
less strangers.

Divided authority too, at best, is ill
understood, or conformed to, by the people of India; and perhaps it may very
fairly be doubted, whether the reformation
introduced by the regulations of 1796, has
tended generally to improve the condition

* Under all those circumstances, it has often happened
that the officers of all ranks, present with their corps, are
not in the proportion of one to each company.

1796. of the Native soldiery, as it regards their satisfaction, contentment, and attachment to the service; or whether they were not better satisfied, upon the whole, under the old patriarchal system of battalions, commanded by a captain, who was always an old officer, experienced in the language, customs, and feelings of the men, which being duly appreciated, never failed to secure respect for authority, and mutual attachment. But it must be remembered, that this becoming consideration for the character and military virtues of the troops requires a progressive course of fellowship and intercourse for its basis.

Other causes are also to be found for a diminished attachment to the service, or rather of the disposition to enter into it, which formerly prevailed amongst the most suitable classes of the community.

That such a diminution has taken place,

there seems little room to doubt. The 1796.
improved condition of their landed property, and the security under which they
enjoy their property in the various pur-
suits and avocations of life, may very naturally have produced such a tendency.
2dly, The harassing, and often offensive
duties, on which the regulars have of late
years been employed, in the situation
which more properly belongs to provincial
corps and police establishments ; in guard-
ing jails, attending convicts on the roads,
or from morning till night in the courts
during the trial of prisoners, with a variety
of other calls to which they are liable
when employed at civil stations, more
especially in the ceded and conquered
provinces, as well as Benares, where the
pressure of such duties has often precluded the annual indulgence of furlough
to visit their families, than which the Na-

1796. tive troops enjoy no higher gratification—these circumstances may no doubt be reckoned on as having likewise contributed to such a result; so irksome and laborious do such duties often prove, that so far from a state of peace being a state of comparative repose, it is quite the reverse; a Maharatta war, or other arduous campaign, is a jubilee to them, compared with the degrading turmoil of such anomalous employment.

It is true, that modifications have at different times been obtained with regard to some of the most offensive duties alluded to, when their feelings could no longer endure the impolitic and malevolent degradation to which they were exposed; but the regret is, that they ever should have been required—for the impression thus made may, as to the effect in question, never be effaced.

A further cause may be stated, and that 1796. a very material one also, in the minds of those concerned. In former times, the men and their families derived a considerable degree of consequence, from some members of the family being in the military service of the company Bahadoor, with this further advantage, that in any case of litigation, injustice, or reference in regard to their agricultural, or other domestic concerns, the influence or consideration derived from their situation always proved gratifying, and generally led to a prompt hearing and decision, without being obliged to wait indefinite and often very protracted periods of time, under the more tardy forms of judicial procedure which have of late years prevailed.

Thus the Sepoy has lost all the advantages, or gratification of that description which he before enjoyed, and with them,

1796. perhaps, some portion of his respect for the character or consequence of his officers, who formerly, by letters of application (now interdicted by an ordinance of the Local Government) to the civil authorities, generally obtained some favourable consideration toward those under their command, when the domestic concerns of the Native officers or men required any such reference. Nor will they soon forget the indignity offered in some instances to their European officers, and to themselves, by the civil process of summons or arrest having been executed within the limits of their camp or cantonments, on individuals against whom complaints may have been preferred, without the observance of any form of requisition, &c. to the commanding officer.

It may be further observed, that in times past the Native commissioned officers, especially the Subadars at the head 1796. of companies, possessed more authority and influence than they now do with their respective companies, in proportion as they were more employed, instead of European officers.

This consequence has further resulted from the change in the interior economy of the corps, by which the more immediate interference in the controul and management of the companies is vested in the hands of the European officers by whom they are commanded and paid: the routine duties of the pay and orderly hawuldars of companies, have necessarily absorbed in a material degree the constant intercourse between the companies and the officers commanding them, of which the Subadars and the Native Adjutant were formerly the link of communication with the officer commanding the battalion:

1796. and hence, perhaps, has arisen a degree of apathy and indifference on the part of the Native officers, especially those who have attained their highest rank, which may more or less pervade the whole machine, by the baneful influence of example.

But it is time to proceed with the narrative of the further services of corps, from the formation of twelve regiments in 1796, down to the present period.

1796-7. Soon after the regiments were formed, as described in the preceding narrative, government resolved on sending a force towards Hydrabad, when the 4th and 10th regiments, augmented by drafts to 1800 privates each, were ordered for that duty, under the command of Major-General Erskine, and the detachment commenced its march from Mednapore early in 1797. On that occasion, a regular supply of camp equipage was for the first time granted to the Native troops of Bengal; a measure 1796-7: for which we may conclude they were primarily indebted to the humane disposition of General Sir Robert Abercromby, who was the Commander in Chief at the time : and thenceforward camp equipage, consisting of light portable sort of tents, was allotted to the whole of the Native army,—that is, for the use of the troops when encamped and marching. No expense is incurred by government for their accommodation, in any other situation whatsoever.

The pay of the Native troops has not undergone any alteration for a long course of years. The private Sepoy receives seven rupees per month in all stationary situations, and eight rupees and a half when marching, or in the field; exclusive of half a rupee per month, allotted to the off-reckoning fund, for which they receive

1796-7. one coat, and nothing more, annually. From that allowance, with which, generally speaking, they are very well satisfied, they not only provide themselves with every thing they require for food and raiment in all situations, but they also erect cantonments for themselves in all stationary situations, at their own expense; and moreover, there are but few amongst them who do not make considerable savings from their pay in the course of the year, which they carry or remit to their families, for their general maintenance and comfort. Indeed, such is the beneficence of their character in this respect, that when they proceed on foreign service, an extensive official arrangement is adopted on the part of government, for remitting to the families and connections of the Native soldiery, a handsome portion of their pay during their absence.

It is further due to their exemplary 1796-7. character and conduct to state, that it is not to their wives and children only that they make such appropriation of a large part of their income; in regard to them it can only be viewed as conforming to an indispensable obligation. But a large portion of the men who have no such ties, voluntarily and cheerfully contribute, in the manner described, to the support of their aged parents, or other more needy relations. Nay, government has been obliged to interpose its authority for restricting the portion of pay which the men might assign to their families whilst on foreign service, in order to obviate the want and inconveniences to which they were otherwise liable to expose themselves in those situations.

Whilst actually on board ship, and in that situation only, their provisions are

s 4

1796-7. supplied at the expense of government, **a** measure which was adopted in the first instance as an encouragement and reward to them for volunteering on such service, and which it has been found equitable and expedient to continue to them, as a sort of bounty and compensation for the great privations and inconveniences to which, as contrasted with their usual habits of diet, cleanliness, and comfort, they are unavoidably exposed while on board ship.

1797. In the month of March this year, Lieutenant-General Sir Alured Clarke succeeded to the office of Commander in Chief.

Early in this year, an invasion of the Upper Provinces was threatened by the forces of Zemaun Shah, King of Cabool. All the troops that could be collected on that frontier took the field under Major-

General Charles Morgan, and all the Native corps were in consequence augmented to a war-establishment by the addition of ten privates per company. Zemaun Shah, however, did not advance farther than Lahore; and when he repassed the Indus, the troops returned to cantonments.

In the month of November, two regiments of Native infantry were added to the establishment, and were numbered the 13th and 14th regiments. The 13th was raised in the province of Benares, and the 14th in the province of Bahar.

In this year the 4th regiment returned from the Northern Circars to Bengal. The 10th regiment proceeded to Hydrabad, from whence, in 1799, it marched to Seringapatnam, and participated in the short and brilliant campaign which put

1798. an end to the sovereignty of the race of Hyder Ally.

The regiment then returned to Hydrabad, and in the year 1800 marched across the continent by the route of Berar, Bopal, &c. to Cawnpoore, where it arrived after an absence from the Bengal provinces of three and a half years. The approbation and thanks of government were expressed in General Orders for the exemplary conduct of this distinguished regiment during its absence on foreign service, and honorary medals were granted to all the Native commissioned, non-commissioned officers, and private Sepoys of the two battalions composing the 10th regiment.

Towards the close of 1798, government called upon all the Native corps of the army for a body of volunteers to the extent of 3000 rank and file, for the pur- pose of proceeding on service to the coast of Coromandel by sea.

The usual inducements of promotion to be made from the volunteers, for the complement of commissioned and non-commissioned officers required for the corps into which they were to be formed, together with the bounty of one month's pay each, were, according to former precedent, held forth on the present occasion.

The requisite number of volunteers were speedily assembled at the Presidency, where they were formed into three battalions of ten companies each, and each company of ninety privates, ten non-commissioned, and two Native commissioned officers. Captains Malcolm, Tetley, and Burrell, were appointed to command the three volunteer battalions, which em-

1798. barked in December, and proceeded to Madras under the command of Major-General Popham.

They joined the army which was in the field preparing to invade Mysore under General Harris, and with their comrades of the 10th regiment shared in the capture of Seringapatnam. Those corps were afterwards employed under Colonel Wellesley, the present illustrious Duke of Wellington, on the northern frontier of Mysore in subjugating refractory chiefs who remained in arms after the fall of Tippoo and his capital.

The Volunteer Battalions marched back by the route of the Northern Circars, and reached Bengal in August, 1800, where they were honoured with the expression in General Orders of the " cordial appro-" bation of government for the distin-" guished services rendered to the British

" empire in India by the European and 1798.
" Native officers and privates of those
" gallant and meritorious corps during
" the late arduous crisis of public affairs."

Honorary medals were likewise conferred on all the Native commissioned,
non-commissioned officers, and privates
of the three Volunteer Battalions, who
were then incorporated as the foundation
of two new regiments on the establishment, as will be hereafter noticed, in the
order of time; on which occasion the
Commander in Chief, Sir Alured Clarke,
was pleased to direct, that in order to
perpetuate the glory acquired by the
Volunteers, each battalion of the new
regiments (the 18th and 19th) should bear
in the upper canton of their regimental
colour, an embroidered radiant star, en-
circled with the words " Bengal Volunteers."

1798.　Towards the close of the year 1798 another regiment was ordered to be raised in the province of Bahar, and to be numbered the Fifteenth; a corps, which, as will be seen in the sequel, soon redeemed the blot which former misfortunes of the service had cast over that number; and fully justified the measure of consigning the stigma to oblivion by authorizing its readmission in the numerical arrangement of the army.

In December, 1798, two more regiments were added to the establishment, and numbered the 16th and 17th. The battalions for those regiments were raised at Juanpoor, Burragong, Gya, and Danapoore. When the 13th, 14th, and 15th regiments were raised, 130 old Sepoys were drafted as a foundation for each battalion of the new regiments, and those men were equally divided between the ten companies, and supplied all vacancies for non- 1798. commissioned officers until the whole were promoted.

This salutary measure appears to have been omitted in the present and all subsequent instances of corps being added to the establishment. Such a foundation, however, was doubtless very desirable, not only for training the levies, but also for supplying vacancies of non-commissioned officers, prospectively, until the corps should be at sufficient maturity to justify promotion in those classes, from the men entertained on the formation of the regiments.

The complement of Native commissioned and non-commissioned officers was always supplied by drafts from all the Native corps of the army by promotion in every rank.

Two non-commissioned officers and fifteen privates were this year added to

1798. each of the ten companies of the Ramgurh battalion.

1800.   In May, 1800, the three battalions of
Volunteers returned from service in Mysore, and were formed into the 18th and
19th regiments on the regular establishment of the army, and to complete those
new formed regiments, men from the
corps disbanded by the Newaub Vizier,
were authorized to be entertained. The
men of the 19th regiment still wear a fea-
ther in their caps (turbans) as a badge of
their honourable origin as volunteers. The
18th declined the option of doing so likewise.

Toward the close of this year, the
Governor-General, Marquis Wellesley,
ordered a division of the Indian army to
embark for Egypt under General Sir
David Baird, for the purpose of co-operating with the army from Britain in the

attack of the French forces on the banks 1800
of the Nile.

A battalion of Bengal Sepoy volunteers
constituted a part of that force, and
sailed from Bengal in December, 1800,
under the command of Major (now Major-
General) E. S. Broughton.

All the ships in which the battalion
embarked did not, owing to stress of weather, reach the port of Cosseir in the Red
Sea, where the troops from India disembarked. But a portion of the corps participated in the honour of passing the
Desert under Sir David Baird, and joining the British army on the shores of the
Mediterranean.

In the month of March, 1801, Lieute- 1801.
nant-General Gerard Lake succeeded to
the office of Commander in Chief in
India.

Another Volunteer Battalion of Se-

T

1801. poys embarked this year under Captain M'Lean, and proceeded to Bombay, intended probably to co-operate with the troops in Egypt, had the war been protracted in that country.

The 1st and 2d battalions of the 6th regiment were employed under the command of Colonel Marley in the hilly and jungly district of Gumsoor, in the vicinity of Ganjam, under the government of Madras. On that service the troops were engaged in very harassing warfare, and suffered great sickness, in subduing a spirit of revolt which had broken out in that quarter.

Hitherto no regular system had been adopted with the Native troops for the duties of light infantry, marksmen, or sharp shooters. Both the flank companies in every Native battalion have always been grenadiers: but the warfare in Eu-

rope, more especially since the French 1801.
Revolution, having proved the great uti-
lity of light infantry troops on all occasions of service, Major-General the Honourable Frederick St. John being one of
His Majesty's general officers on the staff
in Bengal, and consequently in command
of one of the principal divisions of the
army under that Presidency, introduced
the measure with all the corps under his
command of causing ten men to be selected from each company, who were
trained as light infantry and marksmen,
and were denominated sharp-shooters.
Those men still continued on the strength
of their respective companies, but constituted an eleventh company, as it were,
whenever called out to act separately as
light infantry or marksmen, leaving the
battalion formation of ten companies for
field practice, or service, undisturbed.

On a march they were always thrown out by signal as flankers.

This excellent improvement was highly approved by the Commander in Chief, General Lake, who, on a plan being presented to him for forming a rifle corps of Native troops, observed, with reference to the above arrangement, that he thought it a more eligible plan, and meant to adopt it for the whole army; and which was soon afterwards ordered accordingly.

About the middle of this year the Commander in Chief proceeded on a tour of inspection, and fixed his head-quarters at the field station of Cawnpoore.

The Marine Battalion, which was formed in 1795 for the duties of the islands, was this year formed into a regiment on the same establishment as the regiments of the line, and was denominated the 20th, or Marine Regiment.

About the middle of this year the two 1802. Volunteer Battalions returned from Egypt and Bombay; when a trimming reduction took place in the strength of the Native corps—from 90 privates per company they were reduced to 70; thus occasioning the discharge of 400 men from each regiment, or an aggregate of nearly 8000 from the service. The number of non-commissioned officers in each company was likewise reduced from ten to eight.

The volunteers from Egypt were permitted to make choice of the corps they wished to join; the Hindoos were declared exempt from the duties levied on the performance of their religious ceremonies at Gyah, and honorary medals were conferred on all the Native officers, non-commissioned, and privates, who had volunteered on that occasion.

1802.   In the course of this year the Commander in Chief directed that the hawuldars of the Native corps should be armed with pikes instead of muskets. They were likewise ordered to wear pantaloons and sashes, and in all respects to conform to the situation of serjeants in European corps, instead of being included, as heretofore, amongst the rank and file.

1803.   Early in this year a large force was called into the field in consequence of some of the chiefs of districts in the upper part of the Dooaub, recently ceded by the Newaub Vizier, having refused to conform to the regulations and authority of the Honourable Company's administration.

The fort of Saussnie was first attacked, and an attempt to carry it by storm having failed, the Commander in Chief, who was then at Kinouje superintending the disci-

Hawuldar.

Published by I. Murray, Albemarle Street. 1817.

pline of the corps of cavalry, which had 1803. been drawn together for that purpose, repaired in person to conduct the operations of the troops in the field. The strong forts of Saussnie, Bidgygurh, and Cutchoura, were speedily subdued, and the authority of government established over those new possessions. The 1st Battalion 2d, 1st Battalion 8th, the 1st and 2d of the 12th, and 2d of the 15th, were employed on that service, and acquitted themselves highly to the Commander in Chief's satisfaction.

About the middle of the year 1803, a general Maharatta war took place, in the course of which most of the Native corps of the army had an opportunity of participating, in a more extensive degree than had before offered to the Bengal army.

All the corps were augmented to a war establishment of 10 non-commissioned

1803. officers and 90 privates per company. In the month of July the 21st regiment was ordered to be raised, one battalion at Futtehgurh, and the other at Cawnpoore. And in November two more regiments were added to the establishment. The 22d was ordered to be raised at Futtehgurh, and the 23d at Cawnpoore.

In the month of August the Commander in Chief took the field by advancing from Cawnpoore towards the Maharatta frontier in the Dooaub.

Sekundra was the place of rendezvous of corps, where the army was brigaded, and formed in order of battle.

The corps which first took the field with the Commander in Chief were as follows:

1st and 2d Battalions . 2d Regt.
1st and 2d   do.   . . 4th do.
2d Battalion . . . . 12th do.
1st   do.   . . . . . 14th do.

1st and 2d Battalions . 15th Regt. 1803.

4 companies, 2d Bn. . 17th do.

On the 29th of August the army entered the Maharatta territory, and after being slightly opposed by a large body of horse, encamped near the city of Coel.

In the month of September five companies of the 1st Battalion 11th regiment, which were stationed in the cantonments at Shekoabad, were attacked by a large body of the enemy's horse, under a French officer, which had retired from Coel on the approach of the British army; this small body of infantry, with one gun, defended themselves with such effect during a whole day, as to induce the enemy to withdraw from the attack. But having returned the next day in greater force, the infantry retired into the town of Shekoabad, and ultimately the commanding officer was obliged to sign a convention

1803. for the troops under his command not to serve during the war. On those terms they were permitted to march away with their arms, gun, and private property, and the detachment was accordingly ordered to a situation in the interior during the remainder of the war with Scendiah.

On the 4th of September the fortress of Allygurh was carried by assault. The 1st battalion of the 4th, and the four companies of the 17th were the Native troops engaged in that arduous enterprize.

The army advancing towards Dehly was met on the left bank of the Jumna, and in sight of the imperial city, on the 11th of September, by the enemy's brigades of infantry, some cavalry, and a very numerous and well equipped train of artillery. The particulars of that important day, on which upwards of 70 pieces of excellent ordnance were captured, need not be repeated in this place: suffice it to say, that 1803. the corps of Native infantry, which were engaged on the memorable occasion, were the 2d of the 4th, 2d of the 12th, 2d of the 15th, 1st of the 15th, 2d of the 2d, 1st of the 14th, and 1st of the 2d regiments, and honorary standards were conferred on each of those corps, as well as on the 2d of the 17th, of which four companies were also in the action; "in testimony of the pe-" culiar honour acquired by the army on " that occasion." The 1st of the 4th likewise received an honorary standard for its good conduct in the assault of Allygurh, and an extra jemadar was authorized for carrying the honorary standard of each of those corps.

After passing the Jumna, and halting some days at Dehly, the army moved towards Agra, having been intermediately joined by the 1st Battalion of the 12th,

63. the 2d of the 8th, 2d of the 9th, and six companies of the 2d Battalion 16th Native infantry.

On the 10th of October, the six companies of the 16th, the 1st of the 12th, and 2d of the 9th were employed to seize the city of Agra, whilst the 1st of the 14th, and 1st and 2d Battalions of the 15th were ordered to attack the enemy's infantry and guns among, the ravines under the guns of the fortress.

Those services were successfully performed, and all the officers and troops employed were honoured with the expression of the Commander in Chief's approbation and thanks in General Orders.

The siege was then commenced with vigour, and on the 18th of October, the important fortress of Agra, denominated the Key of Hindostan, surrendered by capitulation to the British arms; and the

15th Regiment had the honour of planting 1802. its colours on the royal bastion of the city of Ackbar.

After a few days' repose, during which a distribution of the prize money captured in Agra, amounting to 24 lacks of rupees, was made to the troops, the army advanced into the province of Mewatt, in pursuit of a large division of the enemy's army, consisting of battalions which had arrived from the Dukhun, and had been joined by others from different points of the enemy's possessions in Hindostan, with seventy-four pieces of ordnance, well appointed, and a small body of cavalry.

After a few long marches, for which the season of the year was very favourable, the British cavalry came up with the enemy at day-break, on the 1st of November, 1803, near the village of Lasswarrie, after a march of forty miles in the pre-

1803. ceding twenty-four hours, and the Commander in Chief resolved to make an attack with the cavalry and horse artillery, with the view of detaining the enemy from prosecuting their march through a pass in the Mewatt Hills, until the infantry should come up. This latter object was attained; though the enemy was so strong, and their artillery so well served, that the cavalry suffered severely, and were drawn off by the Commander in Chief until the infantry and guns should come up.

They reached the scene of action about noon, and having marched twenty-five miles, were allowed a short interval to bathe and refresh themselves.

In the mean time, the enemy had formed upon the village of Mohaulpoore, in which their baggage, stores, and bazars were concentrated, covered by their infan-

try and guns, presenting an extensive front 1803.
to the eastward, with their left thrown
back around the northern face of the village, which was situated on a commanding
eminence, with a small mud fort in the
centre, as usual in that part of the
country.

The Infantry was formed in the following order:

The right wing of the army, in open
column of half companies, under the command of Major-General Ware.

His Majesty's 76th, at the head of the
column.

The advanced piquets of the army, consisting of a company from each corps.

The six companies of the 2d Battalion,
16th Regiment.

The 2d Battalion of the 12th.

The 2d Battalion of the 15th.

The 1st Battalion of the 15th.

288

1803. The left wing of the army in the same order, under the command of Major-General the Honourable Frederick St. John, consisting of—

The 2d Battalion of the 8th;
The 2d Battalion of the 9th;
And 1st Battalion of the 12th.

The troops then advanced along the front of the enemy's line, for the purpose of making an attack on their right flank, which was well protected by artillery, and where their small body of cavalry was also posted.

The column having been exposed to a very heavy and destructive fire from the enemy's well served artillery during its advance, the Commander in Chief, as soon as the head of the column reached the intended point, ordered the leading corps to attack and close with the enemy in succession as they came up, rather than

await the operation of a more combined
movement, especially as the progress of
the column had been much interrupted
and delayed by the broken ground, and
by a corps of cavalry, (his Majesty's 29th
Light Dragoons,) which having been ordered to the head of the column, fell in
between the two leading corps, for the
purpose of passing from the left to the
right flank of the column of infantry; the
ground not admitting of their gaining the
head of the column by its left flank, along
which they had previously moved.

The contest at that point was very severe, and for a short time doubtful; but
a gallant charge made by his Majesty's
29th Dragoons, vigorously followed up
by his Majesty's 76th and the Native Infantry corps at the head of the column,
supported by the Battalions of the 15th,
decided the tide of battle, and the enemy

1803. gave way; still, however, continuing to do execution with their artillery, at different points of their position, until they were completely broken, and obliged to retire, which they did in a very sullen manner, after throwing themselves into a solid mass; leaving the whole of their guns, stores, bazars, &c. in the hands of the victors.

During the contest in forcing the enemy's right, the veteran General Ware had his head carried off by a cannon-ball, and was succeeded in the command of the wing, at that crisis, by Colonel, now Lieutenant-General Sir John Macdonald, K. C. B. and the heroic Commander in Chief, General Lake, having been at the head of the column the whole time, had two horses shot under him.

From the plan of attack adopted on this occasion, it necessarily followed that

the corps which were more immediately 1803.
engaged, and suffered most in the battle
of Lasswarrie, were those whose situation
in the column of march brought them first
in contact with that point of the enemy's
position against which the attack was directed; and in the Commander in Chief's
order of thanks on the occasion, the six
companies of the 16th, under Lieutenant-
Colonel, now Major-General Sir H. White,
K. C. B. and the 2d Battalion of the 12th,
under Major, now Colonel R. Gregory,
C. B. were the corps of Native Infantry
specially noticed, for their timely and gallant advance to the support of his Majesty's 76th.

The enemy having been defeated as
above stated, by the column composed of
the corps of the right wing of the army,
before those of the left wing arrived at the
point of attack, the latter had no further

1803. participation in the action than what resulted from their sustaining some loss from the enemy's cannonade, during the march of the column.

Our loss in this battle was very considerable; but it was decisive, and closed the campaign in that part of India, by the defeat, capture, and dispersion of all the corps and field equipments in the service of Dowlut Rao Scendiah in Hindostan.

Soon after the firing had ceased, many men of the enemy's corps, relying on the humanity of the English officers, and the sympathy of their countrymen, a great portion of the troops in the two armies having been natives of the same provinces, sought refuge from the cavalry pursuit by gathering about the Native Battalion left on the field of battle to collect the wounded men and the captured ordnance, and throwing down their arms, they were screened with 1803. the mantle of generosity, from the becoming feeling, " that an enemy subdued is an enemy no more."

Such was the insufficiency of our hospital equipments, compared with the number of the troops wounded in the battle of Lasswarrie, that the men of the Native corps were called upon, and cheerfully undertook the office of carrying their wounded brethren, during the return-march of the army, until they could be lodged in the hospitals within our own frontier.

Whilst this rapid and brilliant course of events was proceeding, under the personal guidance of the Commander in Chief, other corps were in the field on various points of the frontier.

Lieutenant-Colonel P. Powell entered the province of Bundelkund with the 1st

1803. Battalion, 13th; 1st Battalion, 18th; and other details.

The 2d Battalion, 7th, and a detachment of the 20th, or Marine Regiment, were employed in concert with troops from Madras, in seizing the province of Cuttack; and the Ramgurh Battalion was actively employed on the frontier toward Naugpoore.

A force under Lieutenant-Colonel George Ball, consisting of the 1st Battalion 8th Native Infantry, with two battalions formed from the corps which had lately been in the service of Scendiah under European officers, and some auxiliary horse and foot, was employed in subduing the forts of Narnoul, Kanoon, &c. and establishing the authority of Government in the districts on the Dehly south-west frontier, which formed part of the Maharatta assumed possessions in Hindostan.

Lieutenant-Colonel W. Burn, with the 1803. 2d Battalion 14th, and some auxiliary troops, was employed in gaining possession of the country at the head of the Dooaub, and dislodging a predatory force from Karnaul and the adjacent districts.

All those officers and troops were distinguished by a spirit of professional exertion and successful enterprize, which called forth the particular approbation and thanks of the Commander in Chief, and of the Government.

In the month of December, a force under the command of Lieutenant-Colonel, now Major-General Sir Henry White, K. C. B. was detached from the main army to attack the fortress of Gwallior.

The six companies of the 2d Battalion 16th, the 2d Battalion of the 9th, and the

1803. 1st of the 14th, proceeded on that service, and were joined by the 2d Battalion 11th, and 1st and 2d Battalions of the 18th, from the division of the army in Bundelkund, which had been progressively augmented with several regular battalions, and a large force of irregulars formed from corps which had been recently in the service of the enemy in that province.

The siege of Gwallior was vigorously pressed, and the garrison soon surrendered by capitulation.

The end of this year, two battalions of Volunteer Sepoys were formed at the Presidency, and embarked for Ceylon, under the command of Lieutenant-Colonel Hunter and Major George Dick, for the purpose of aiding his Majesty's Government in that colony, in the war in which it was engaged with the King of Candy.

Although the forces and power of 1803.
Scendiah, in Hindostan, were finally disposed of by the battle of Lasswarrie, on
the 1st of November, the army still
continued in the field, under the Commander in Chief, and at the close of 1803,
moved to the pass of Biana, where it remained encamped six or seven weeks,
watching the motions of Jesswunt Raow
Holkar, who was threatening an irruption
into the Company's territories.

The beginning of this year, the main 1804.
army under the Commander in Chief,
moved into the Jeypoore country, for the
purpose of protecting that state, and to
intercept the forces of Holkar, in the event
of their penetrating in that direction.

The fort of Rampoorah, which belonged
to Holkar, was carried by assault in a gallant manner, by a detachment from the
main army under the command of Lieu-

1804. tenant-Colonel Don, in which the 2d Battalion 8th, and 2d Battalion 21st, were engaged, and were afterwards left to garrison that place.

The army remained in the sandy regions of Jeypoore until the near approach of the rainy season, when the Commander in Chief withdrew the corps into cantonments, within the frontier of the Honourable Company's possessions, leaving three excellent battalions, viz. the 2d of the 2d, and the 1st and 2d Battalions of the 12th Native Infantry, with a handsome equipment of artillery under the command of Colonel Monson, to watch the motions of Holkar, in concert with the Jeypoore Government.

About the middle of this year, a disaster befel the division of the army in Bundelkund, where half a company of European artillery, and three companies of Sepoys of the 18th Regiment, which had been 1804. detached from the main force, were surprized by a party of horse under the orders of Meer Khan, an active partizan of Holkar's, and were all either killed or taken prisoners; and some pieces of ordnance, with which they were endeavouring to reduce a fort, were also carried off by the enemy. After which, Lieutenant-Colonel Martindell was appointed to command that division of the army, with which the following battalions were engaged in a variety of arduous service, and had to contend with very severe sickness during the course of that and the following year: the 1st Battalion 1st Regiment, the 2d of the 6th, the 2d 11th, 1st of the 13th, 1st and 2d Battalions 18th, and perhaps other corps, which may have escaped recollection.

In the course of the year, a still more

1804. serious disaster befel our arms, by the retreat of Colonel Monson's detachment.

Colonel Monson, after increasing the force under his immediate command, as above specified, by the junction of the 2d Battalion 8th, and 2d of the 21st, from Rampoorah, (leaving some details from those corps for the duty of the fort,) advanced with his detachment into Malwa, to a position fifty miles to the southward of the Mokundra pass.

The fort of Hinglauzgurh, belonging to Holkar, was attacked and carried by assault in a gallant manner by the 2d Battalion 2d, under Major Sinclair; but shortly afterwards, in the beginning of July, Holkar advanced with a powerful force of horse, infantry, and artillery, and the detachment was ordered by Colonel Monson to commence its retreat towards the Company's territories.

The periodical rains had set in with 1804. great violence, and the detachment was soon obliged to abandon all their guns, which, of course, fell into the hands of the enemy.

The sufferings of the troops, from the want of provisions, exposure to the rains, and the pressure of the enemy harassing their march, were extremely trying and severe. Suffice it to say, they continued to retreat under accumulating distress and disaster. On reaching Rampoorah, they were joined by the 2d Battalion 9th, and 1st Battalion 14th, which had been ordered to push forward from Agra to their support. Colonel Monson, however, did not deem his force sufficient to keep the field against the enemy; nor could any adequate supply of provisions be obtained; it was therefore resolved to prosecute the march until they should reach

1804. the fortress of Agra, the nearest point of refuge on the frontier. The retreat was accordingly resumed, leaving the 2d Battalion of the 8th, and four companies of the 2d of the 21st, to garrison Rampoorah, under the command of Captain Hutchinson of the Artillery.

The 2d Battalion 2d, the 1st and 2d Battalions of the 12th, the six companies of the 2d of the 21st, and the 2d Battalion 9th, and 1st of the 14th, with two howitzers, now constituted the retreating corps: surrounded by large bodies of the enemy's horse, they generally moved in an oblong square, sustaining and repelling the frequent charges made by the enemy's horse with a degree of resolution and firmness which could not be surpassed by any troops, in any climate.

On the plains of Hindown, the country being particularly favourable for the ope-

rations of cavalry, the enemy's horse, 1804.
amounting to 20,000 or upwards, formed
together, after clearing an extensive wood
and ravines, and immediately separated
into three bodies, for the purpose of making a general attack upon the retreating
corps, before they had resumed the formation of the square, which was scarcely accomplished, when the enemy charged on
all sides with the greatest impetuosity; but
the cool intrepidity of the troops preserved
their honour and their lives. Not a mus-
ket was fired until the enemy was within
a few paces, when many of them fell close
to the ranks, and a few individuals finished
their career within the square. When the
smoke and dust cleared away, the men
cheered their officers on the result of this
determined effort on the part of the enemy,
and hoped they would repeat their attempt. But though a fine plain presented

1804. itself during the whole of that day's march, the enemy shewed no stomach for such another reception, until the evening, with the aid of large bodies of freebooters from the hills, when they made another trial of their fury, but with no better success than before.

At the passage of the Bunass river, prior to the occurrence above stated, the 2d Battalion of the 2d, with the piquets of the line under the gallant Major Sinclair, and Colonel Monson, who was also present, were nearly annihilated, having been attacked by the enemy after the rest of the detachment had crossed the river. They repeatedly charged and captured several of the guns which the enemy brought against them, but at length, overwhelmed by numbers, they were obliged to yield to their fate, and sealed their service to the state with their lives ; but very

few, either officers or men, having escaped. 1804.
The loss of the detachment at large, in killed, wounded, and missing, during the retreat, was very considerable. The remains of those gallant corps reached Agra the end of August, in a very shattered condition. The retreat of that detachment, in regard to the event itself, was necessarily viewed and felt at the time as a public misfortune. But on no occasion, perhaps, did troops ever deserve greater honour and reward. Their determined valour, steady discipline, and their perfect obedience to authority under the pressure of the most aggravated difficulties and distress, during a retreat for a continued period of eight weeks, through a hostile and barren country, surrounded and incessantly assailed by a victorious and cruel enemy, may, with truth, be affirmed to have established a claim to the most

x

1804. exalted reputation, which will redound to the honour of the Bengal army to the latest period of its existence. For further particulars of that retreat, see Appendix H.

It remains to be added, that the enemy left no means or offers untried, through the medium of intrigue, to induce the troops to swerve from their allegiance and fidelity, during the pressure of the retreat; and the promises of reward and advancement were accompanied by threats of the most dreadful vengeance upon all who, not availing themselves of those offers, should afterwards fall into the enemy's hands; a threat which was very fully executed in various instances afterwards.*

* It was confidently reported at the time, that a surgeon, and some European artillery-men, who fell into the enemy's hands, were murdered under Holkar's personal inspection. Intoxicated with victory and cherry-brandy,

Under such circumstances, the bribes 1804.
held forth made some impression, but in
a very limited degree, and that chiefly,
it was understood, in the two battalions
which went from Agra to the support of
the corps which originally composed the
detachment, and from which some desertions in consequence took place. On the
return of the corps to Agra, some of the
Native officers were tried for having encouraged or connived at the intrigues of
the enemy. Some of them were pronounced guilty, and were sentenced to
suffer death, but they were pardoned by
the Commander in Chief.

he caused those unfortunate men to be brought before
him, and after making them an offer of service, which
they declined, he ordered their heads to be smashed to
atoms with the wooden mallets used for driving tent-pins;
and most of the Sepoys who fell into his hands were muti-
lated by the loss of their nose or right hand.

x 2

1804.   Officers and troops having been obliged to abandon, or throw away their baggage, in the course of the retreat, the Honourable the Court of Directors were pleased, on the representation of the Commander in Chief and the government of Bengal, to grant two months pay and batta to the Native troops, as a compensation for their losses on the occasion. The European officers were likewise allowed compensation according to the rules of His Majesty's service in that respect, and a further grant of three months full batta to each, in consideration of their sufferings and meritorious conduct.

Following up his tide of flood, Holkar did not draw bridle till he reached the banks of the Jumna, where, as he was said to have observed at the time, he had long wished to regale himself, in the sacred bowers of Muttra and Bindrabund.

The Commander in Chief, however, 1804. soon made him get into his saddle again. Corps were assembled at Agra with the best practicable expedition, whither his Excellency repaired by rapid marches from Cawnpoore. In the meantime Holkar had detached his infantry and a very extensive park of artillery to besiege Dehly, then occupied by the 2d battalion of the 4th, 2d of the 14th, and four companies of the 2d of the 17th Native infantry, under the command of Lieutenant-Colonel W. Burn, at which time Lieutenant-Colonel Ochterlony was the Resident at the imperial court on the part of the Company's Government, having been placed in that situation by the Commander in Chief, after the battle of Dehly.

As soon as a force was in readiness to move from Agra, of which the following

1804. Native infantry corps formed a part, viz. the 1st and 2d battalions of the 12th, and the 2d of the 21st, composing the reserve; the 1st battalion of the 4th, 1st of the 8th, 1st and 2d of the 15th, 1st of the 21st, and 2d of the 22d, the Commander in Chief moved towards the enemy, and after having in vain endeavoured to bring Holkar and his cavalry to action in the vicinity of Muttra, his Excellency prosecuted his march towards Dehly for the purpose of raising the siege of that place. Holkar with his cavalry swarmed around the British army during the whole of the march from Muttra to Dehly, molesting its progress, and destroying its supplies by every means which a great superiority in cavalry force and their desultory mode of warfare enabled them to practise with vexatious audacity.

On the near approach of the British

army to Dehly, the enemy raised the 1804. siege, and retired with their infantry and guns through Mewatt, till they took up a position near the fortress of Deeg, belonging to the Raja of Burtpoor, who, encouraged by Holkar's success, entered into alliance with him against the English government.

The defence of Dehly reflected great credit on Lieutenant-Colonel Burn, who commanded the troops; on Lieutenant-Colonel Ochterlony, the Resident; and on all the officers and troops, whose conduct was distinguished by the most animated zeal and laborious exertions in the defence of the imperial city, and the descendants of the house of Timoor; for which they received the most cordial approbation and thanks of the Commander in Chief, and the Government.

Holkar with his cavalry pushed across

1804. the Jumna to carry fire and sword into'
the Company's possessions. The Commander in Chief divided his army, proceeding in person with the greater part of
the cavalry force, and the infantry reserve
above-mentioned, inclusive of the flank
companies of His Majesty's 22d Foot, in
pursuit of Holkar down the Dooaub ; and
after the extraordinary march of 252 miles
in thirteen successive days, having in the
last two days marched upwards of 54 miles
within 30 hours, they surprized Holkar's
cavalry under the walls of the city of Fur-
ruckabad.

The 2d of the 14th, and 1st of the 21st,
having been previously detached into the
Dooaub under Colonel Burn, were obliged
to throw themselves into the fort of Sham-
lie, in which they were blockaded by
Holkar's cavalry until the Commander in
Chief's approach made them decamp.

The remainder of the army, under Major-General Fraser, countermarched from
Dehly down the right bank of the Jumna,
in pursuit of the enemy's infantry and
guns; and on the 13th of November was
fought the battle of Deeg, in which the
1st Battalion of the 2d, 1st of the 4th, 1st
of the 8th, the 1st and 2d Battalions of the
15th, and the 2d of the 22d, were engaged,
and were highly distinguished by their
steady discipline and effective valour.

This was perhaps one of the hardest
fought battles during the war, and our
loss was proportionably great. Between
80 and 90 pieces of ordnance were captured, inclusive of most of those which
fell into the hands of the enemy during
the retreat of Colonel Monson's detachment; and likewise some of the battering
guns, which were given to the Maharatta
confederates, by Earl Cornwallis at Se-

1804. ringapatnam, after the peace concluded there in 1792.

On the arrival of the Commander in Chief, and the force with which he had been pursuing Holkar in the Dooaub, the siege of Deeg was commenced, in which the corps engaged in the previous battle were employed, as well as those constituting the reserve, viz. 1st and 2d Battalions of the 12th, and 2d of the 21st, which had accompanied the cavalry in pursuit of Holkar.

The town of Deeg, which was strongly fortified, and a commanding out-work, were carried by storm, and the citadel was then evacuated by the enemy.

In September, 1804, orders were issued by Government for the addition of four more regiments of infantry, which were numbered the 24th, 25th, 26th, and 27th.

The 24th and 26th were raised at Cawn- 1804. poore; the 25th and 27th at Futtehgurh: and to expedite the formation of the new corps, for which the exigencies of the time were very pressing, the provincial corps, which had been raised for the internal duties of the ceded and conquered provinces, were ordered to furnish large quotas of drafts, and officers were ordered to raise additional levies at Allahabad, Lucnow, Purtauhgurh, and Sooltapoor. For a particular anecdote of the 25th, (2d Battalion,) see Appendix H.

After the fall of Deeg, the end of De- 1805. cember, 1804, the army moved to the siege of Burtpoor, leaving the 1st of the 4th to garrison Deeg.

The attack of Burtpoor continued during the months of January and February, and in the several assaults made on that place, the 1st and 2d Battalions of the

1805. 12th, 1st and 2d Battalions of the 15th,
1st of the 2d, 1st of the 8th, and 2d of the
22d, highly distinguished themselves by
their spirited exertions and steady discipline; and although their endeavours
were not ultimately crowned with the
success to which they so well entitled
themselves; it is but a tribute of impartial
justice, unquestionably due to those corps,
in common with the rest of the troops
employed on that arduous service, to declare, that their character acquired additional lustre and renown from the persevering gallantry and zealous devotion
which they eminently displayed under
circumstances of unusual discouragement,
and the repetition of numerous and afflicting casualties.

It is justly due to the 2d Battalion of
the 12th regiment to insert in this place
the following quotation from the General

Orders by the Commander in Chief, 1805. after the failure of one of the attempts made to carry that place by storm.

" Notwithstanding the distinguished " and persevering gallantry displayed by " the troops in the assault of yesterday, " and that the colours of .the 2d battalion " 12th regiment, were three times planted " on the top of the bastion, the obstacles " were such as not to be surmounted."

On that occasion, when a retreat was ordered, it was with great difficulty the men could be prevailed upon to withdraw; they yielded at length to the reiterated orders of their officers, after having repeatedly exclaimed, " We must take " the place, or die here." Too fully was their determination verified, for in several of the corps employed, more than half their number were either killed or wounded.

1805. From Burtpoor the army moved across the Chumbull to watch the motions of Scendiah's forces in that quarter, but no particular service occurred, and the troops returned to canton for the rainy season within the frontier of the Company's possessions, leaving a force of two or three battalions, under Lieut.-Colonel Bowie, in the province of Gohud, where some hostilities took place, the particulars of which, as to the troops more immediately engaged, cannot now be recollected with sufficient accuracy to specify further particulars in this place.

Towards the close of the year, the Commander in Chief again moved in pursuit of Holkar, who, having rallied a force during the rainy season, penetrated by the Dehly frontier, and passed the Sutludje, into the Punjaub. Thither he was speedily followed by Lord Lake, and

after a very pleasant march, and the en- 1805.
joyment of a fine renovating climate, the
British army of India was encamped at
Christmas, 1805, on the banks of the
Hyphasis, where Alexander formerly
terminated his march towards India;
and where a treaty of peace having
been concluded with Holkar under the
dictates of political, not military necessity, the operations of the war finally
terminated, and the troops returned to
the dominions of the Honourable Company. A short time previous to the
commencement of the Maharatta war,
a small corps, consisting of three companies of pioneers, was raised, for the first
time, under the Presidency of Bengal.
They proved of the most essential service
during the war, and were highly distinguished for their gallantry and prowess

1805. on many trying occasions, under the command of Lieutenant Swinton.

As far as memory now serves, the prominent services of the Native infantry corps during the Maharatta war have been enumerated. Various other services of distinguished enterprize and professional gallantry were doubtless performed during that eventful period, but which could not be adverted to without entering into a minutiæ of detail foreign to the object of this brief Narrative, which is intended only to record the characteristic features of the Native troops, and the prominent services of the Sepoy battalions on the establishment of Bengal. Nothing has been intentionally omitted which comes within the scope of the object above stated. The records of the Bengal government afford ample testimony of the professional

character, collectively and individually 1805.
maintained by the Native troops of Bengal, during successive periods of time, and especially throughout the war of 1803-4-5, in the course of which there occurred a more general field for exertion and enterprize, than had before fallen to the lot of the Bengal army. See Lord Lake's Farewell Orders, Appendix I.

It can hardly be necessary to add to the foregoing observation, that it is by no means intended to insinuate that all the important actions which have been briefly referred to in the course of this Narrative were achieved by those corps *only* which have been particularly noticed; but that such is the history and relative circumstances of service of the different battalions of Sepoys, in continuation of the first part of this little tract, in which the rise and progress of corps has been so accurately

Y

1805. described. Neither, on the other hand, does this sketch profess to render an account of *all* the services performed by the Native troops of the Honourable Company's Bengal army—any such attempt would require volumes to do them justice; for in those extensive dominions, from the banks of the Sutludge in the north to the Chilka Lake in the south, never a year passes but some corps, detachment, or minor details of troops are employed on field service, involving as much exposure to the casualties of warfare, and affording full as great a scope for the early display of the spirit of professional enterprize and exertion, as occurs in any other military service whatsoever. In the Vizier's dominions our troops are more or less employed every year on service which must necessarily be very painful to their feelings; in enforcing

the exorbitant demands of the Vizier's collectors of the revenue, and subduing forts
and fastnesses, often of great strength
and difficulty, to which the subordinate
renters are frequently driven in despair to
resist the faithless exactions of the renters
of districts and provinces; and thus, as if
no bounds were to be set to the tests of
their fidelity and obedience, are the Native troops often required to exercise military hostility against their own families,
relations, and friends; for the proceedings
above stated are carried on in the very
provinces from which two thirds or more
of the Native officers and men composing
the Native infantry corps are recruited.

The termination of foreign war brought
with it, in the early part of this year, the
usual mortifications of reduction, retrench-
ment, and reform. The companies of
Native Infantry throughout the army were

1806. reduced to 80 privates each; and all the Local, or Provincial Battalions, which had been raised for the internal duties of the ceded and conquered provinces, inclusive of that at Benares, were ordered to be disbanded, and the Native commissioned officers of them were thrown as supernumeraries upon the regular corps of the army. This, however, was a burthen which the operation of time would soon remove. But a much more offensive burthen was thrown upon the Regulars, by assigning to them the performance of the various irksome, disgusting, and harassing duties under the civil authorities of districts, for which Local Corps, or details, on an inferior footing of pay, &c. had hitherto been employed throughout the provinces under the Bengal Presidency. But we must proceed, in the order of time, to draw to a

conclusion the History of the Native 1806.
Corps.

In the beginning of this year several 1807.
strong forts were reduced in Koonch and
Bundelkund by a detachment under the
command of Lieutenant-Colonel Haw-
kins. The fort of Chameer was carried
by assault at noon-day, on which occasion
the 2d Battalion of the 1st, and 1st Battalion of the 16th, were distinguished.

In the month of February the army had
to lament the departure for Europe of
their gallant Commander in Chief, Lord
Lake, under whose personal command in
the field they had established a proud
and lasting reputation for professional
gallantry and personal attachment and
devotion to the service of the Company
Bahadoor. An interregnum ensued, during which the office of Commander in
Chief was administered by three different

1807. General Officers, when towards the end of the year, Lieutenant-General George Hewett arrived and entered on the command in virtue of his appointment from Europe.

In the course of this year, a large force was again in the field, under the command of Major-General Dickens, to subdue the fort of Komona, &c. in the Dooaub, in consequence of the renter by whom they were possessed having placed himself in a state of resistance to the civil authorities of the Honourable Company's government.

The 1st Battalion of the 9th, 1st and 2d of the 13th, 1st of the 23d, 1st and 2d of the 27th, and from which a Grenadier Battalion was formed, were the Native Infantry corps employed on that service. The fort of Komona was defended with the most determined resolution and bravery, and our loss in officers and men 1807. were very considerable, both in the European and Native corps which were engaged. The Pioneer Corps was likewise there, and distinguished themselves, officers and men, as usual; and, as usual, sustained numerous casualties.

The small body of pioneers was this 1808. year organized, as far as regards the Native part, into a regular corps of eight companies, of 90 men and two European Serjeants each, besides a detail of miners attached, and was thenceforward denominated the Corps of Pioneers or Sappers. But the European officers, in the proportion of two to each company, are only borrowed from the regiments of the line, as in the instance of the Ramgurh, and other Local Corps. It was notified in General Orders, that under the formation now adopted, the Pioneer Corps was to

1808. be considered as raised to the same honourable level, as the other corps of the Company's regular army, and that it was to be governed by the same rules and regulations in all respects, as are established for the corps of Native Infantry.

In the course of this year, the Bengal government resolved to take military occupation of the island of Macao in China; and a battalion of Volunteer Sepoys was called for as a part of the force to proceed on that service.

The requisite details were soon furnished accordingly by the corps which were in the vicinity of the Presidency, where they were formed into a battalion, and embarked under the command of Major F. R. Muller.

They landed at Macao, and remained there some months under circumstances of restraint and mortification very trying

to their feelings, but to which, in obedience to the example and injunctions of
their officers, they submitted with their
characteristic deportment of forbearance,
and decorum; and on their return, in
1809, the special approbation and thanks
of government were expressed in General
Orders for their exemplary conduct on
that expedition.

Owing to various causes of delay, the
honorary colours granted to corps engaged
at the battle of Dehly in 1803 were not
formally presented until this year.

On the 1st of November, the 15th regiment, being then at the Presidency, had
the honour of receiving the honorary
standard for each battalion from the hands
of Lord Minto, the Governor General.
For his Lordship's speech on the occasion,
See Appendix K.

In the course of this year, a regular

1808. establishment of light infantry was introduced into the Native corps of the Bengal army. The two flank companies were continued, grenadiers, as before, and the 1st Battalion company was ordered to constitute a light infantry company in every battalion throughout the service.

That measure was followed by the light companies of the army being called out, and formed into separate battalions of light infantry, for the purpose of being trained in the light infantry evolutions and practice; after which, the several companies were, early in 1809, ordered to rejoin their respective corps, with the exception, for a while, of the 4th Light Infantry Battalion, under Major B. H. Kelly, which was employed on active service in Bundelkund.

1809. The Commander in Chief was on a tour of inspection, and superintending military

Light Infantry Sepoy.

Published by I. Murray. Albemarle Street. 1817.

preparations on the north-west frontier, 1809. with reference to the probability of French invasion, in alliance with the Court of Persia.

Some of the Sikh chiefs had likewise shewn indications of hostility, and a large force was accordingly assembled in Sir-hind, which ended in a post being established at Loodhiana, on the left bank of the river Sutludge, where three battalions of Native infantry, with a regiment of cavalry and artillery details, cantoned, under the command of Lieutenant-Colonel Ochterlony.

A large force was likewise still on service in Bundelkund, under the command of Lieutenant-Colonel Martindell; and early in this year, the strong hill-fort of Adjiegurh was captured, after a smart affair on the heights of Ruggowly, in which the 4th Light Infantry Battalion, and the

1809.   1st Battalion of the 18th, were prominently engaged.

About the middle of this year, a brilliant exploit was achieved by a force under Lieutenant-Colonel George Ball, in subduing a turbulent and hardy race in the province of Hurriana, whose boast it was, that they had never submitted to the regular controul of the authorities which had presided over that country. The province of Hurriana came under the Honourable Company's Government, consequent to the Maharatta war of 1803 and 1804: the inhabitants continued their lawless habits, and recently had the audacity to plunder the baggage of a detachment of the Company's troops, which passed near their principal strong-hold of Bhawannie.

The 1st Battalion of the 9th, the 2d of the 18th, the 1st of the 22d, and 2d of the 23d, were the battalions of Native 1809. infantry employed on that service. The difficulty of the undertaking was much enhanced by the scarcity of water, which is rarely to be found any where in that part of the country but within the walled towns. It was therefore in the rainy season only, that the service could be attempted with any prospect of success.

The detachment having encamped near the fortified town of Bhawannie, and made an offer of terms of submission to the inhabitants, which they refused to accept, the place was attacked and carried by assault in a very gallant manner, on the following day, by which such a salutary impression was made on the minds of the rude tribes inhabiting those distant territories, that a proper respect for the authority of Government has since been duly observed by them.

1809.   In this year, the companies of the Marine Regiment were augmented to sixteen non-commissioned officers, and one hundred and thirty privates each, so as to render each battalion adequate to furnish the details required for the duties of Penang, Malacca, and Sumatra, and thus enable the two battalions of that regiment to effect a complete relief of each other alternately, on the Island duties; a measure which the previous strength of the corps rendered impracticable.

1810.   The middle of this year, two battalions of Volunteer Sepoys were required to proceed on an expedition against the Isle of France.

The 1st and 2d Battalions of the 8th, the 2d of the 12th, the 1st of the 15th, 2d of the 19th, and 1st and 2d Battalions of the 25th, having been the corps nearest to the Presidency at the time, speedily fur-

nished the complement of volunteers re- 1810.
quired; and two battalions of the established strength were formed, under the
command of Major Burton, and Captain
Lumley.

They embarked at a very unfavourable
season of the year, and had a boisterous,
tardy voyage; they arrived just in time,
however, to participate in the capture of
that colony, to the no small annoyance of
the French troops and colonists, who observed, that to be subdued by British
troops was one thing; but to have the
black fellows of India sent against them,
was an indignity which no subject of his
Majesty the Emperor and King could
endure with any patience.

After the capture of the island, the Volunteer Battalions remained some months
to assist in keeping Monsieur in good
order; and the general good conduct of

1810. the troops whilst on that service, redounded greatly to the honour of both officers and men, as may be seen by the General Orders by the Commander of the Forces at the Mauritius, on the occasion of their departure from the island. For copy of which, see Appendix L.

At the close of the year, five more battalions of Volunteer Sepoys were called for, to constitute part of the force to be employed on an expedition for the conquest of the Island of Java, which had fallen under the dominion of France. On that occasion all the Native infantry corps of the army were allowed to furnish a quota of Volunteers, with exception to the Marine Regiment, and those battalions which had recently sent forth handsome details against the Isle of France.

The two Battalions on that service having been denominated the 1st and 2d

Battalions of Bengal Volunteers, those 1810.
now proceeding against the Island of
Java were formed into five battalions,
and numbered in continuation the 3d,
4th, 5th, 6th, and the 7th, or Light
Infantry Battalion of Bengal Volunteers,
which were assembled and embodied at
the Presidency with the most commendable alacrity; whence they embarked in
the spring of 1811, under the general command of Colonel George Wood. The
following officers were appointed to the
command of the battalions: Lieutenant-
Colonel M'Grath; Major Dewar; Major
Raban; Major P. Grant; and Captain
Dalton.

The volunteers for Java, after enduring 1811.
a long and irksome detention on ship-
board, at length landed at Batavia early
in August, 1811; and it appears from the
concurrent accounts of their conduct on

z

1811. that arduous service, on which the 2d Battalion 20th, or Marine Regiment, was likewise employed, that they nobly maintained and enhanced the reputation of the Bengal Infantry,—" Having by their stea-
" diness and gallantry in action, and by
" their discipline and good conduct in all
" situations, excited general admiration
" and esteem."

Instances of their individual bravery and prowess, when opposed to European troops, were likewise mentioned in the accounts from the Island. For notice of which, see Appendix M.

Thus, in the year 1811, the Bengal army had the honour of having sent forth seven battalions (or 7,000 men) of Volunteer Sepoys, on service beyond sea, to co-operate in wresting from the power of France the possessions held by that government to the eastward of the Cape of Good Hope.

Such a draft, however, could not be 1811. spared without great inconvenience and pressure of duty on the several corps of the army. Levies for supplying the place of the Volunteers were accordingly ordered to be raised with all practicable expedition. By the end of the year, the two battalions returned from the Isle of France, and the men rejoined the corps to which they before belonged.*

* One of the battalions (the 3d) appears to have returned from Java to Bengal in 1815, when it received the thanks of Government in the most handsome terms, for their beneficial services and good conduct. The other battalions having been thus long detained, (far beyond the' period contemplated when they embarked,) they will probably remain until the restoration of the colony to the Government of Holland; and thus will those troops have established additional claims to admiration and applause, by having cheerfully continued to serve for a protracted period of more than five years, in a distant, foreign country, where they necessarily endured many privations, and suffered much sickness and mortality. Since the capture of the island, they have frequently been engaged on service in Java, and adjacent islands, particulars of which, it is to be hoped, will be recorded hereafter.

1811. In the course of this year, General Hewett returned to Europe, and was succeeded in the office of Commander in Chief by Lieutenant-General Sir George Nugent.

1812. Early this year, the important fortress of Kallinjur, the capital of the province of Bundelkund, was attacked, and surrendered to a force under the command of Lieutenant-Colonel Martindell, after an attempt to carry it by storm had been repelled by the garrison.

The following Native Infantry corps were employed on that service :—

The 2d Battalion, 2d Regiment,

2d . . of the 5th ditto,

1st . . of the 7th ditto,

1st . . of the 11th ditto,

2d . . of the 11th ditto,

And 2d . . of the 16th ditto.

The Ramgurh Battalion was augmented

to twelve companies, and the strength of 1812. companies increased to one hundred rank and file each. For a remarkable instance of intrepidity on the part of a Sepoy of that corps, see Appendix N.

A further detail of one thousand Volunteer Sepoys embarked for Java, to fill up vacancies in the five Volunteer Battalions serving in that island.

In the month of October, General the 1813. Earl of Moira succeeded to the united office of Governor General and Commander in Chief.

This year closed with a brilliant little affair, by a detachment employed in Buggailkund, under Lieutenant-Colonel J. W. Adams. The fort of Entourie was stormed and carried, after a most desperate resistance on the part of the garrison. The Chief, who had been guilty of acts of wanton aggression towards a detachment of

1813. the Company's troops, when he found that resistance was no longer of any avail, threw himself into a house filled with combustibles, and thus burnt himself to death. Details from the 2d Battalion 2d, 1st Battalion 5th, 1st of the 9th, 2d of the 10th, and 1st of the 11th Regiments, were engaged in this affair. For which see London Gazette, in the year 1814.*

1814. In the course of the year 1814, the Bengal Government having been forced into war with the state of Nepaul, by a series of aggressions on the part of the

---

* The following particulars are from an officer who was present. The garrison consisted of about one hundred and fifty men: they fought in the breach for an hour and a quarter like tigers. When the place was nearly carried, the enemy set fire to it in several places, making the whole a sheet of fire,—they still kept fighting in the flames, till the Chief blew himself up. This was a hard day's work; we were under arms marching, breaching, and storming, upwards of twenty hours. Not many of the garrison escaped; a few of the wounded survived, and shewed us the remains of their Chief.

officers and troops of that predatory 1814.
Government, three regiments of Native
Infantry were added to the establishment,
and numbered the 28th, 29th, and 30th,
making a total of thirty regiments of
Native Infantry, of two battalions each,
which, on an average, yields the addition
of one regiment per annum since the organization of the army into twelve regiments, by the regulations of 1796.

The corps of Native Infantry, throughout the service, were augmented to ninety
privates per company. Grenadier and
light infantry battalions were formed ; and
several local corps were raised for the
internal duties of the provinces.

A large portion of the army was engaged on very arduous service during the
Nepaul war; but sufficient information
and particulars have not yet come to
hand, to admit of their being detailed in

1814. this place. It is, however, to be hoped, that the conduct and services of the corps engaged in that war will be hereafter recorded, in continuation of this feeble attempt to preserve the history, and appreciate the character and merits, of the troops composing the East India Company's Native Infantry army, on the establishment of Bengal.

In that hope, the present sketch is now closed by subjoining the following brief, but impressive testimony, addressed in a letter from Bengal to this country, by an impartial observer during the Nepaul war in 1815.

" We cannot sufficiently admire the " Bengal Sepoys; such gallantry, submis- " sion, temperance, and fidelity, were per- " haps never combined in any soldiers."

The writer of this brief continuation, or Supplement, cannot take leave of the

subject without many pangs of regret, 1814.
heightened by the apprehension, that it
may never again be his good fortune to
serve with troops, who are endeared to
him by a companionship of service, and
professional exertion in various situations,
during a period of more than thirty years;
to whom he is proud to offer the tribute
of his grateful attachment and affection;
and of whom he can conscientiously declare his conviction, (adopting the words of
Mr. Hastings, quoted in the Appendix,)
" under the most solemn appeal of religion,"
that with treatment of the most simple and
practicable tenor, the characteristic qua-
lities of gratitude, attachment, fidelity,
cheerful obedience, and respectful deportment of the Native soldiery of Bengal,
must ever reflect lustre on their moral
and military virtues, and may be justly
held forth as a theme of emulation and
praise to all mankind.

Comrades of my early youth, and of the best portion of life, which has been cherished and rewarded through the medium of your meritorious conduct,

FAREWELL!

<hr>

NOTE.—The custom which prevailed in former times, of calling corps by the name of the officer who raised, or who commanded them for a series of years, has been gradually falling into disuse, with regard to all corps raised since the establishment was condensed into twelve regiments, in 1796. All the battalions of those old corps still retain their original appellation: but the practice could no longer be observed with the same degree of propriety or effect, with regard to corps raised since that period, which, under the fluctuating circumstances of the service in regard to commanding officers of corps, compared with the different state of things in former times, are generally described by the Natives as the Right (1st) or Left (2d) Battalion of regiments respectively; which are expressed by their numerical arrangement.

APPENDIX A.

A List of the Officers of the Bengal Army, in the Year 1760.

CAPTAINS.

John Gowan
Thomas Fenwick
James Spear
Christian Fisher
5 Martin York
Ranfur Lee Knox
Peter Carstairs
Charles Earnest Joecher
Alexander Champion
10 Henry Oswald
Hugh M'Kie
Thomas Robertson
Lauchlan M'Lean
Giles Stibbert
15 Henry Spelman
Martin White
James Tabby
18 Patrick Moran

CAPTAIN-LIEUTENANT.

1 John Broadburn.

LIEUTENANTS.

William Turner
George Wilson
Ambrose Perry
Henry Sommers
5 Hugh Grant
John Nollickens
Christian Hasencliver
John Mathews
Francis Cozens
10 Anthony Casteel
John Price
James Treadwell
John Trevanion
Sir William Hope
15 Lewis Brown
John M'Dowall
William Ellerson
John Downie

George Alston
20John Bourne
  William Smith
  Primrose Gailliez

George Morrison
Gilbert Ironside
James Morgan
26John White

Ensigns.

Anthony Polier
Richard Parry
John Mauve
Thomas Fenwick
5William Glenn
Archibald Swinton
Walter Furlong
George Hay

Samuel Hampton
10Maurice Roach
Benjamin Wilding
James Jones
Richard Holland
John Walkins
15John Mackleron

Total Officers—60.

At present there are upwards of 1600 officers on the military establishment of Bengal.

NOTE.—It appears by a memorandum with Captain Williams's manuscripts, that in the year 1756, immediately preceding the capture of Calcutta by the Newaub Suraja Dowlah, the officers and troops in the service of the East India Company, in Bengal, consisted as follows :—

In the garrison of old Fort William,

Infantry - - - - - 145 } inclusive of officers.
Artillery - - - - - 45 }
_____
190

Of that number 60 only were Europeans, the rest were native Portugueze, dressed as Europeans, and called Topasses.

About 200 of the latter description were detached at the subordinate factories of Cossimbuzar, Dacca, Luckypoore and Ballasore, but they could not reach Fort William before it was invested.

The troops in the Fort were commanded by Captain Minchin, commandant; Captains Clayton, Buchanan, Grant, and Witherington commanding the artillery. Captains Minchin and Grant accompanied Governor Drake to the ships, some days before the Fort surrendered; the former was dismissed, but the latter returned to the service, and served under Clive at Plassey. Captains Clayton, Buchanan and Witherington died in the black-hole.

The lieutenants and ensigns were as follows:—Lieutenants Bishop, Hays, Blagg, Simsom and Bellamy; Ensigns Piccard, Scott, Hastings, Wedderburn and Walcott. All of whom, except Mr. Walcott, perished in the black-hole; and Mr. W. died shortly after. Ensigns Carstairs and Muir were detached at the out factories, and thus escaped the miseries of the black-hole.

APPENDIX B.

PROCEEDING from Calpee, the detachment lost, on the second day's march, one of its most valuable officers, Captain James Crawford, commanding the 4th battalion, who died from a stroke of the sun. Connected with that unfortunate event, the following relation of facts will doubtless be read with unfeigned sympathy and admiration.

Captain Crawford had acquired the character of an excellent Sepoy officer, and the battalion which he com-

manded was considered one of the finest corps in the
service.

The appellation of Crawford, by which the 4th battalion was called by the men of the corps, and the natives
in general, was an exception to the practice that generally
prevailed in former times, of calling corps by the name of
the officer by whom they were formed, or that of the place
at which they were raised.*   Captain Crawford was considered by the men as a rigid and perhaps severe disciplinarian, yet that excellent officer so happily blended, with
the strictest principles of military discipline and arrangement, the practice of the most inflexible integrity and
impartial justice, in the general exercise of the influence
and powers of authority, combined with considerate and
manly indulgence, in regard to the religious habits, the
customs and prejudices of the men under his command,
that of Captain Crawford it may with truth be affirmed,
he had the good fortune to verify what ought to be the
emulation and object of every military man, with regard
to those under his command, the enviable distinction of
commanding their lives through the medium of their
affections.

It is a fact no less creditable to Captain Crawford's
memory, than it is honourable to the character of the men
whom he commanded, that during the halt of the detachment at the encampment where he was buried, (which

* The 4th battalion had been raised and commanded by other
officers previous to Captain Crawford; but the professional pride
and ambition which he felt on succeeding to the command of the
corps, made him anxious to have it called after his own name, which
he accomplished, not without some trouble in the first instance; but
which his subsequent conduct sealed and confirmed for ever!

continued for several days, owing to the severity of the weather and waiting the arrival of stores, &c. from Cawnpoore,) all the individuals of the corps, Native officers and men, went from time to time to render their tribute of grateful attachment and affection, by making their obeisance, after the manner of their country, at the grave of their lamented commander. And on the day the detachment moved forward from that encampment, the grateful and sorrowing Crawford, or 4th battalion, after it had been told off preparatory to the march, requested leave to pile their arms, and to be permitted, collectively, to go and express their last benedictory farewell over the remains of their respected commander, protector and friend.

What soldier can read this without being inspired with a resolution to emulate the example, and aspire to the honour which distinguished the character and exalted the memory of Captain Crawford! or emphatically to exclaim, in the language of Scripture, " May my last end be like his."

APPENDIX C.

General Order issued by the Commander-in-Chief.

Fort *William*, 25th Feb. 1785.

MINUTE BY WARREN HASTINGS, ESQ. GOVERNOR-GENERAL, DATED 1st FEB. 1785.

THE Governor-general, having been precluded, by the distance of the last station of the detachment lately returned from service in the west of India, from making his acknowledgments in person for their exemplary services, and being now on the eve of departing for Europe, requests the Commander-in-chief to publish to the officers, his countrymen, and to the native officers and Sepoys of the different corps which comprised that detachment, his thanks for the distinguished honour which their gallant and persevering spirit and splendid successes have reflected on the government over which he presided, and on himself in particular, for the share which he had in their original appointment; for having under that appointment restored the lustre of the British arms; for having successfully attempted and achieved a long and perilous march through hostile and unknown regions, from the banks of the Ganges to the western coast of India, and proved by their example that there are no difficulties which the true spirit of military enterprize, under British conduct, is not capable of surmounting.

The Governor-general desires also to avail himself of the same mode to take his final leave of the army in general, to whom he shall deem himself bound in honour to afford, wherever and whenever required, his testimony of their collective and separate merits, for all have occasionally entitled themselves to his thanks; and to declare, as he most conscientiously does, even under the most solemn appeal of religion, that the British arms have, in no part of the world, better sustained their genuine character than those of the establishment of Bengal.

(Signed)   WARREN HASTINGS.

APPENDIX D.

*General Orders by the Government of Bengal,
dated Fort William, the 22d of January, 1785.*

THE Governor-general and Council direct, That their
thanks be expressed in General Orders to Colonel Pearse
and the European officers, and the Native officers and
privates composing the detachment lately returned from
the Carnatic, for their gallant behaviour and useful services in the defence of the Company's territories in the
Carnatic during the course of a long and unequal war;
and as a lasting mark of their approbation, they bestow on
each of the Sepoy regiments a pair of honorary standards;
on each of the subadars a gold medal, and on each of the
jemadars a silver one, with such a device, motto and
inscription as shall be judged applicable to the occasion;
and medals of the same sort to the officers of the Gholundauz company; also similar badges, of inferior value, to
such of the men, warrant-officers and privates as have
served with the detachment from the commencement of
the expedition until its return into the provinces.

The Governor-general and Council further direct, That
in acknowledgment to the services of the two great
detachments which have served in the Carnatic and the
west of India, an additional pay of two roupees per
month be granted to each non-commissioned officer and
private of the European corps;* and one roupee per

* The Honourable Company's 1st regiment of European infantry
of the Bengal establishment, as well as European artillery details,
were detached to aid the presidency of Fort St. George in the war
with Hyder Ally. They were eminently distinguished for their
valour and efficiency throughout that arduous war; of the former,
their veteran commander-in-chief, Sir Eyre Coote, observed, on

54 PPENDIX.

month to each non-warrant officer and Sepoy of the
Native corps composing those detachments who were
originally attached to the same, on the march to their
respective destinations, and returned with them.

This additional pay to commence from the first of the
present year.

General Order, by Warren Hastings, Governor-General.

Camp at Ghyretty, January 25th, 1785.

The Governor-general, having already testified his sense,
in the General Orders issued by the Governor-general and
Council, of the meritorious conduct of the corps lately
returned from the Carnatic, can add nothing to the credit
of their services by any acknowledgment which he, as an
individual, can make to them; yet they will not be displeased to receive from him the separate tribute of his
particular and personal thanks, for his share of the reputation which their actions have reflected on the government of Bengal, in its original appointment of the detachment to the relief of the Carnatic.

Great as the exertions have been, which were made by
the gallant troops employed on that service, it will in no
degree derogate from them to affirm, That to this aid the
Company's possessions and interests under the presidency
of Fort St. George owe their present existence; and that
with every report made to this government of the successes of the war, the most honourable mention was

some occasion of a feu de joie, which they did not execute very cor-
rectly—" D——n those fellows, they are good for nothing but
fighting."

uniformly made of the Bengal detachment, as primarily distinguished by its patience of hardship, its generous submission to the pressure of those wants which affected every corps of the service, but which were to them, acting at such a distance from their native homes, the cause of aggravated distress; by its steady discipline, activity, and effective valour.

The Governor-general has deemed it incumbent upon him to visit the detachment in person, to offer his thanks to them before their separation; and desires that the commanding officer, whom he is proud to call his friend,* will make them known in public orders to the officers, his countrymen; and to the Native officers and private sepoys of the detachment.

The term of his public existence is now within a few days of its close. But it is a consolation to him thus to mix with his regrets, for the loss of a service endeared to him by many years of care, attachment and vicissitudes, a declaration of justice and gratitude marking its last period. (Signed) WARREN HASTINGS.

Minutes of Council, 26th January, 1785.

The following Minute, by the Governor-general, being so consonant to the ideas of the other Members, and so creditable to himself, they requested and obtained his Permission for the Publication of it at length, in General Orders.

THE GOVERNOR GENERAL.

The detachment sent from this presidency to the relief of the Carnatic consisted, in its original formation, of above

* Colonel Thomas Deane Pearse, of the Bengal artillery.

5,000 men; and is now reduced, by the service it has seen, to less than 2,000. These small remains being returned to Ghyretty, the Governor-general yesterday visited their encampment; and he hopes that the Board will allow that indulgence to his feelings, excited by the mixed sentiments of gratitude and regret, which were impressed by the occasion, as to accept with candour the following recommendation which it has induced him to make in their behalf:

The Board have liberally rewarded the services of the Native officers and privates of the detachment, and afforded such testimonies of those which have been rendered by the European officers, as will be felt by men professing the spirit of honour which they have so signally displayed, with sentiments superior to such as are excited by the pledges of substantial bounty,—neither is it easy to devise others. Such additional honours as may be bestowed, the governor-geveral now begs leave to recommend; and these are, as follows:

1st. That a sword be given to Colonel Pearse, the commanding officer of the corps, and one to each of the lieutenant-colonels his second and third in command, Lieutenant-Colonel Edmonstone and Lieutenant-Colonel Blane, both as a testimony of their faithful and meritorious services, and for the incitement of example to others their juniors.

2dly. That the officers who are now attached to the corps, in whatever degree of command, may be confirmed in their stations and commands, notwithstanding the general rules of appointment. Such an indulgence will be equally grateful to the officers themselves, and to the men who have served with them, as the removal of the former, for the sake of a literal adherence to general rule, would appear like the privation of the right, which the chance of hard and severe service has given to the surviving officers of the detachment, in favour of others who have enjoyed a long season of repose; and would be a cruel separation of the sepoys from the officers to whom' they are endeared by their common sufferings, and operate as a more cruel hardship, by placing them under strangers, to whom their merits will be unknown or unfelt.

3dly. That the names of the officers be entered on record, for such future marks of the favour of government as the rules of the service may admit; and to this list may be joined, on the same principle, that of the officers who have lately served with the other great detachment returned from the other side of India.

This is the last appeal which I shall make to my present colleagues in the administration; and I venture to declare, without consulting them, that the sentiments of one are similar to my own, from the same impulse, excited by the personal meeting with men so deserving, and among them some veterans who were once his associates in the same career of military enterprize; and that those of my successor* will be not less favourable, when, to the spirit of liberal discernment, he shall have joined the same personal motives as those which I have ascribed to myself and Mr. Stables.†

      (Signed)   WARREN HASTINGS.

* Sir John M'Pherson, Bart.
† John Stables, Esq. member of council—formerly in the army and commanded a battalion at the battle of Buxar.

APPENDIX E.

Extracts from Mr. Hastings's Narrative of the Insurrection which happened in the Zeemeedary of Benares, in the month of August, 1781.

" On my arrival at Chunar, I found myself in great and immediate distress for want of money. The troops were some four, and others five months in arrears; and as the Rajah Cheyt Sing had the country on all sides at his devotion, I had not the smallest prospect of obtaining supplies, until the motions of our troops from different quarters should open a communication: I have, however, great pleasure in testifying that, distressed as the Sepoys were for the want of money, they never manifested the least symptom of discontent. I frequently visited the camp, and passed the lines each time in review: once, and only once, I heard one or two voices of complaint, but neither clamorous nor disrespectful.

" Whatever judgment may be passed on my particular conduct, I am yet happy that it has proved the means of calling forth the inherent virtue of my countrymen, and displaying to all the powers and people of India, both the national character, and the national constitution, by such effects as have been unrecorded in their histories, and are scarce conceivable by their habits of thinking.

" The suddenness of our calamities; the distance of assistance; the privation of every present resource; the manifest interest which animated and impelled every corps, and every individual, to the support of the common cause; and the rapidity with which they rushed to repel the common danger,—are facts of universal observation; and will contribute more effectually to the permanency of the British influence and dominion than the most splendid victories obtained over adversaries of the highest reputation; because they shew the harmony which unites all the parts of our government, and their augmented strength under the compression of external violence;— and will be remembered as a most striking example, which every man concerned in its operations will apply to his own interests and feelings, that its greatest and most successful exertions have arisen out of the most desperate emergencies, and have fallen, in every such instance, with the most dreadful vengeance on the heads of its aggressors.

" The same spirit animated every officer of every corps, and infused itself into the men under their command, with an effect so far exceeding the common occurrences of human affairs, that in the short space of one month, this great and valuable province, which had been suddenly and wholly lost, was in substance wholly recovered to the British empire."

After particularizing the meritorious services of officers and corps, Mr. Hastings concludes as follows:—

" Such have been the spirited and judicious exertions of your officers and troops, in support of the Company's most valuable rights and possessions, of the dignity of their Government, of the honour and safety of their Chief Magistrate: a conduct which manifests the strongest attachment and affection on their parts, and implies an observance of justice and regard to the prosperity and happiness of those who are placed under our authority, on ours.

" These are circumstances which will always afford me

A A 4

the most pleasing reflections, notwithstanding the calamities which have produced them."

The following observations may be appropriately added, in illustration of the foregoing testimony.

Let it not be forgotten, that on the critical occasion of the revolt of Cheyt Sing, and the provinces under his controul, the fidelity, attachment, and devotion of the Native soldiery to their sense of duty, was inherent, spontaneous, and undisguised ; for had the shadow of any other feeling found place in their minds, there was no European force employed on that service, nor near at hand, which could for a moment have overawed or controuled the conduct of the Native troops : the only European details having been, as before mentioned, the two flank companies of the 2d European Regiment, a small portion of artillery, and the company of Foreign Rangers ; and of the latter nearly half were killed and wounded, in the rash attack and failure on the town of Ramnagurh.

The following anecdote, connected with the warfare to which the Benares insurrection gave rise, is worthy of being added.—It is contained in one of the affidavits in the Appendix to Mr. Hastings's Narrative, before quoted.

The spirit of revolt and hostility toward the English Government soon spread itself over the provinces of the Vizier's dominions, which were contiguous to those of the Zeemeedary of Benares.

The corps in the Vizier's service, which were commanded by English officers, (lent for the purpose from the Company's army,) in some instances mutinied, and were disposed to join the insurgents ; whilst other detachments and parties remained faithful to their officers, and taking refuge in forts, &c. exerted their efforts to oppose the torrent of hostility and sedition.

The affidavit states, that the fort of Ghoruckpoor was attacked by near six thousand rebels; there was a Jemadar (Native officer) and about fifty men in the fort, who behaved most gallantly. The attack commenced near nine o'clock in the evening; they carried the outer fort, which was too extensive, and the party were obliged to retire to the citadel, where there were upwards of two hundred prisoners confined: they endeavoured to seize the Sepoys, in which attempt nineteen of the prisoners were put to death, and many wounded. The attack continued till near four o'clock in the afternoon, when Shawmut Khan, a jemadar, and nine men, who had been ordered to march there from Puroonah at the beginning of the disturbances in the country, arrived in the town; the people told them to throw down their arms, and run off to the jungles to save their lives, for it was impossible for them to get into the fort, as it was surrounded by six thousand rebels, who must carry it in a few minutes.

The Jemadar, with admirable presence of mind, replied, that he was only the advanced party, and that the Captain with the Battalion and the guns, were close after them,—called out to a man to run and bring them up, that the whole of the rebels might be destroyed,—and immediately fired upon the rebels. The report instantly spread, a panic seized the whole, and they ran off in the utmost confusion. He joined the party in the fort with his nine men: they sallied out after the rebels, and cut off about two hundred of them. During the attacks, the rebels frequently called out to the Jemadar to deliver up the place to them, as they had Perwanahs from the Begum, Cheyt Sing, and Sadutt Ally, for what they did,

APPENDIX F.

General Orders, by Earl Cornwallis, Commander in Chief, on the return of the Eight Battalions of Bengal Sepoys from the war in Mysore.

Fort William, 23d January, 1793.

THE Commander in Chief congratulates the detachment on its return to the Bengal provinces, and desires that before the separation of the corps that compose it, Lieutenant-Colonel Cockerell will convey to them, severally, his hearty approbation of their conduct upon the service upon which they have been employed with so much glory to themselves, and benefit to the public.

In the course of that service he had frequent occasions to commend their patience under fatigues and difficulties, and their gallantry in action ; and he has now only to add, that the adherence and fidelity of the Native officers and soldiers on a service so extensive in its duration, and so distant from the Presidency to which they belong, will be a memorable proof of the attachment of the Bengal Native soldiery to the British Government in India, and will ever reflect the highest credit on the European officers through whose just and conciliatory treatment that attachment was obtained and preserved.

To the Native officers and Sepoys composing the Volunteer Battalions, and to the Volunteers dispersed through the corps of the detachment, the Commander in Chief desires that his peculiar satisfaction may be expressed, for the alacrity with which they offered themselves to join the army engaged in an arduous and remote war, by a conveyance so much at variance with their feelings and inclinations. It is a pleasing reflection to him, that during his government, a spirit has been shewn by the Native soldiery of sacrificing their prejudices to their duty, and of overcoming their natural reluctances when the state has occasion for their services; and he trusts that the example set by the Volunteers, of embarking on board ship, and the reports which they will spread among their fellow soldiers of the great care and attention bestowed by Government, and the officers of ships, to render their situation during the voyage as comfortable and commodious as possible, will completely remove from the minds of the Native soldiers in the service of the Company, that aversion to sea voyages which so long prevailed amongst them.

It is positively enjoined to commanding officers of battalions to which the Volunteers will be distributed, that they pay particular attention to the merits of those men, and hold in remembrance their claims to promotion, when opportunities occur.

The conduct of Lieutenant-Colonel Cockerell in the field, of Major Russell, and the other staff officers of the detachment, and of commanding officers of corps, was on different occasions noticed in terms of strong approbation in the General Orders to the army, and the Commander in Chief has great pleasure in now declaring, that Lieutenant-Colonel Cockerell, in the general command of the detachment, has manifested so unremitting an attention to the care of the men under his charge, and to the important object of economy in public expenses, as to entitle him to the fullest approbation and thanks of Government; whilst the accounts received from every quarter,

of the orderly behaviour of the troops during the march
to and from Madras, as well in our own countries as those
of our friends and allies, are unquestionable proofs of the
discipline and regularity which has been maintained in the
detachment.

(Signed,)   P. Murray,
Adjutant-General.

Issued in Camp, on the southern bank of the Sooban
Reeka River, 25th January, 1793.

APPENDIX F.

Detachment Orders, by Lt. Colonel Cockerell.

Camp South of the Sooban Reeka River,
· 21st January, 1793.

The detachment being arrived on the southern boundary of the Honourable Company's Bengal Provinces,
the place of rendezvous of corps, in March, 1790, and
where Lt. Colonel Cockerell had the honour to enter on
the command, he embraces the occasion to congratulate
officers and troops on their return from a very long and
arduous foreign service. It has been a service that admitted of exertions of military ardour and gallantry, which
will give a lustre to their reputation more than usually
occurs: and the proof these Native corps have evinced
of attachment to their colours is not less conspicuously
creditable, than is the willing zeal they displayed on every
occasion where their services were commanded during the
late war with the Sultaun of Mysore.

The very commendable conduct observed by the troops in all intercourse with the inhabitants of the districts in the route of the march, the Commanding Officer is authorized to speak of from his own observation: but he possesses the additional satisfaction of public acknowledgments from the Chiefs of Settlements, Collectors, and Renters, in terms of thanks and high praise of the behaviour of the detachment, and which Lieutenant-Colonel Cockerell has this day preferred to Earl Cornwallis.

The corps composing the detachment will separate to their respective destinations from this encampment. Lt. Colonel Cockerell therefore takes this opportunity to declare to the officers and soldiers, that he shall ever retain the most perfect esteem for their merits.

The testimonials published in the General Orders of the Grand Army, whilst serving in Mysore, by the Right Honourable Earl Cornwallis, of the ardour, the obedience, and the patience under fatigues of service, which these corps manifested, are so recent, that Lieutenant-Colonel Cockerell would deem it superfluous to retrace those occasions in any Orders by him; but he has adverted to them that he might express in this public manner his own personal acknowledgments to the corps: a sentiment which naturally presents itself to his mind, from having had the honour to be their Commanding Officer during a service that has added to their military reputation, and which he entreats of Commanding Officers to explain to their corps in his name.

Lieutenant-Colonel Cockerell hopes that Major Russell, his second in command, and the commanding officers of battalions, will be assured that he entertains the highest sense of their unwearied attentions to the corps, and of the support they have invariably afforded him in the duties of his command. He has had the peculiar happiness to see his orders obeyed with a promptness and zeal which scarcely required the coercion of the powers annexed to command; a zeal certainly founded on the first military principles, " confidence, and respect for authority;" but to which he has the pride to believe, a third principle obtained some influence; a regard to his station in the public responsibility of command : it is a proof of their friendship that will make a lasting impression on his memory, and claims his most sincere thanks.

To the European officers in general, and staff, Lieutenant-Colonel Cockerell wishes to acknowledge the very sensible pleasure with which he has observed their invariable endeavours united to promote the harmony of society since the formation of the detachment; the singular success resulting therefrom redounds no less favourably to their private stations than is their public conduct honourable to their official capacities.

(Signed)   EDMUND WELLS,
Major of Brigade.

APPENDIX G.

The following Account of the Action of the 26th of October, 1794, is copied from the Calcutta Gazette.

Camp Rampore, 26th October, 1794.

THE whole line was ordered to be under arms this morning an hour before daylight; the General and his staff moved to reconnoitre some miles in front; they saw the enemy forming in full force; and after waiting some time to judge of the probable disposition they would take, rode back to camp to direct the arrangements for action. Our army moved forward in line, the artillery in the intervals of corps, the cavalry on the right flank; the charge of the enemy was most daring and gallant, and it is utterly impossible it could have been surpassed; both lines met, and intermingled. The bayonet at length prevailed, and our army pursued the enemy across the Doojoora rivulet. The enemy was said to have consisted of 25,000 men, of which 4,000 were cavalry, who directed all their efforts against the reserve, and made dreadful execution. The number of the enemy killed was great. Our loss in European officers was very afflicting. Major Bolton was shot, after having cut down several of the assailants.* His battalion behaved with a degree of steadiness which would have done honour to the most disciplined corps in the world.

The charge on the part of the enemy was particularly singular; they formed in line, infinitely beyond the extent of ours, in deep wedges, supposed of 50 deep. When the signal for our advancing was given, we moved in good order, slowly forward, at that time about 1200 yards from the enemy. They likewise moved towards us. When the lines were within about 500 yards of each other, Gholam Mahomed's people scattered individually, approached in that extraordinary manner, and contested the point with our bayonets. They appeared to despise our

* Major Bolton commanded the 18th Battalion. He was a remarkably large, powerful man.

musketry; and upon every discharge of artillery, embraced the ground, instantly rising again, and advancing
to the charge; their arms were spears, matchlocks, and
swords, which latter they employed with destructive effect, and their attack, as by universal consent, was called
the Highland Charge.

APPENDIX H.

IT was about the middle of July, 1804, that the retreat
commenced; and with the exception of the short halt
under the walls of Rampoorah, where the troops had
some little repose, the men endured the greatest hardships
and privations with heroic firmness, and perfect obedience
to authority.

The whole of the camp-equipage was abandoned at the
Mokundra pass, on the third day of the retreat. From
that time the troops had no shelter whatsoever from the
elements, nor any provisions but what they could find in
the deserted villages which were contiguous to the route
of the detachment. Many of the men were without
shoes, performing long and harassing marches by day and
night, from twelve to twenty-four hours together, constantly surrounded by large bodies of the enemy's horse,
attacking, or making demonstrations of attack, from time
to time; and frequently making use of their light artillery,
which could not be replied to, the whole of the guns of
the detachment having been spiked and abandoned in the
early part of the retreat. The rainy season was at its
height, so that the flooded state of that quaggy country
rendered the marching doubly fatiguing; and when the

troops were allowed intervals for halting, they had not any shelter, nor a dry spot to rest upon.

Every mode of bribery, intrigue, and terror, was practised by the enemy to withdraw the Sepoys from their allegiance. Money was offered, promotion, &c. was promised to all who would quit their colours, and give up their officers; with threats of the most cruel treatment to all who should fall into the enemy's hands; a threat which was most inhumanly verified in many instances afterwards.

As soon as any of the enemy's spies were discovered, they were seized by the men, and brought to their officers, to whom they urged the propriety of shooting them without further ceremony.

Under the influence of despair, more than any other motive, it was conceived, some few desertions did take place; but the instances were few indeed, considering the dilemma to which those gallant troops were reduced.

The enemy's cavalry was so numerous, that the troops were obliged to march in a square wherever the country admitted of that order being preserved; this increased the restraint and fatigue of the march : but the security and confidence which it yielded, made the men conform to it with the utmost precision and alacrity.

The men were often heard to express their wish that General Monson would halt, and wait the arrival of the whole of the enemy's army, when they would be answerable with their lives to put him in possession of all the enemy's guns.* At other times they would express their

* The enemy's cavalry with some light artillery were pressing the retreating troops, whilst his infantry, and a very extensive park of artillery were following.

B B

agony and mortification, that the reputation which they had acquired under General Lick (Lord Lake) should be tarnished by a retreat, which would never have taken place, if their wishes could have prevailed.

In consequence of the swollen state of the rivers, owing to the periodical rains, the retreat of the detachment was impeded for several days on the banks of a rivulet between Kotah and Rampoorah, and which they were at length compelled to cross under circumstances of the utmost difficulty, in order to avoid starvation. The only mode that could be resorted to for getting the troops across was by making rafts from such wood as could be got from the roofs of houses in the neighbouring villages; and by making the elephants swim to and fro with as many men as they could carry at a time. But a dreadful scene of confusion and disaster ensued; rafts crowded with men went down before they reached the opposite bank; and when the elephants became tired from swimming across so often, they frequently in the midst of the stream shook all who were on their backs into the river; most, or all of whom perished. Towards night most of the troops had crossed or perished; but most of the camp followers, soldiers' wives, children, &c. remained on the opposite side. till morning. Those unfortunate creatures had no protection; and during the night, bands of robbers and freebooters from the hills attacked, plundered, and massacred many of them; whilst their cries were heard by their husbands, fathers, &c. on the other side of the river, who were tortured into a state of despair and frenzy. It was with the utmost difficulty the officers could prevent the men from throwing themselves into the river under the influence of their agonized feelings. Sentinels were posted along the bank for the purpose, but notwithstanding, several men, it was understood, lost their lives in that dreadful manner.

· At the passage of the Banass river, on the 24th of August, when the troops composing the rear guard, consisting of the 2d Battalion 2d Regiment, and the piquets of the line, under the gallant Major Sinclair, were nearly annihilated by the overwhelming force which the enemy brought against them after the rest of the detachment had crossed the river, and could render the rear-guard no support, large bodies of the enemy's horse having also crossed the river to keep them in check, a remarkable instance of heroism and devotion was displayed by a Subadar or Jemadar of the 2d of the 2d, who was seen from the opposite side of the river, retiring with a stand of colours in one hand, and defending himself with the other, until he reached the bank of the river, into which he plunged, but sunk with the colours, to rise no more.*

Exhausted and broken down as the gallant remains of this unfortunate detachment were, when they reached Agra, on the 30th August, and following days, (for from the Biana pass to Agra, a distance of about 50 miles, there was no longer any connected order of march preserved,) the troops no sooner heard that Lord Lake was pressing forward with such corps as could be collected, for the purpose of checking the enemy's career, than they all expressed the most earnest desire to be speedily equipped for the field, that they might have an op-

* The colours of the Native battalions, of which there are two stands with each corps, as in His Majesty's service, an union and a regimental colour, are always carried by Native commissioned officers.

portunity of revenging the sufferings to which they had been exposed.

The Commander in Chief, in testimony of his sympathy and perfect conviction of their meritorious conduct, ordered the 1st and 2d Battalions of the 12th, and the 2d Battalion of the 21st, being the three corps which were first re-equipped, to join the army in the field, and appointed those corps with the flank companies of his Majesty's 22d Foot, to constitute the reserve of the army under his Lordship's personal command; in which situation they had the honour of accompanying the cavalry during the laborious marches for thirteen successive days, in pursuit of Holkar's cavalry from Dehly to Futtehgurh.

N. B. The position from which the detachment commenced its retreat was upwards of 350 miles from Agra.

The Official Account of the proceedings of the detachment, from the 7th of July to the end of August, was published in the Calcutta Gazette Extraordinary of the 2d of October, 1804.

APPENDIX I.

The following affecting circumstances relating to the 2d Battalion 25th Regiment are so honourable to the memory of Captain Charles Christie, by whom that corps was first raised and formed; and at the same time such a noble illustration of the characteristic virtues and feelings of the Native Soldiery of India, that, being in possession of the authenticated fact, it would be unpardonable to omit its insertion in this place.

THE 25th regiment, with others, as has been stated, was raised towards the close of 1804, and Captain Christie was selected for the duty of raising and forming the 2d battalion of that regiment at Futtehgurh.

So inadequate was the previous strength of the army to the demand for troops, occasioned by the arduous and widely extended warfare in which the government of India was then engaged, that it was necessary, very early in 1805, to bring those young corps forward, to co-operate with the army engaged in the field.

Meritorious and indefatigable as were the exertions of all the officers who were employed in raising and forming those corps, it will be no disparagement to them to declare, that the 2d of the 25th, under Captain Christie, surpassed the others by its more early appearance of military efficiency and perfection.

Captain Christie was blessed with that happy beneficence of disposition which made it his constant practice and delight to blend paternal kindness and conciliation with the requisite exercise of authority as an officer.

To use the words of an eye-witness, " Captain Christie had raised, clothed and disciplined the corps with all the tenderness of a parent, and all the solicitude and pride of a soldier: the commander and the men were proud of each other. But he had barely accomplished this first wish of his heart in bringing the corps to maturity, when he was seized with a violent illness, which, in a few days, deprived the corps and the service of a valuable and exemplary officer.

"Captain Christie died on the 30th of April, 1805, and was buried at Saintree, on the left bank of the Jumna, between Agra and Muttra. The Native officers of the corps, so contrary to their customs and religious prejudices, solicited permission to carry the corpse of their beloved commander to the grave: the whole corps followed the mournful procession with a general countenance of affliction and grief, presenting one of the most affecting scenes I ever beheld. After the funeral ceremony each sepoy stepped forward to look into the grave, threw a clod of earth on the coffin, and retired in melancholy silence; the whole corps sorrowing in tears."

A similar instance of grateful attachment and respect for their commanding officer was since evinced by the 2d Battalion of the 3d Regiment, on the death of Lieutenant-Colonel John Foster, at Dehly, in May, 1811; which is also well worthy of being recorded in this little memoir; and is therefore copied accordingly from the Calcutta Government Gazette :—

Died at Dehly, on the 11th instant, (May, 1811,) Lieutenant-Colonel John Foster, commanding the 2d Battalion 3d Regiment of Native infantry.

" This worthy and lamented man was beloved and esteemed by all who had the happiness of knowing him. He was an affectionate husband, a tender father, and faithful friend: a zealous and valuable officer; and a strict, yet temperate, disciplinarian.

" As a last mark of affection to his person and veneration for his memory, the sepoys of his battalion entreated to be allowed to carry his remains to the place of interment: their wish was complied with, and they bore his coffin to the grave.

" The solemnity of the funeral procession, the unfeigned sentiments of sorrow depicted in the countenances of the whole of the troops in garrison, consisting of two battalions and five companies of sepoys and the artillery brigades, which attended the funeral, were greatly affecting."

Men, who, by such noble conduct, exalt the character of their nation amongst foreign tribes and in distant regions of the globe, may indeed be said to deserve well of their country; and to be entitled to its best distinctions and rewards. But whether such be their recompense or not, they will derive a still higher gratification in the consciousness of having well fulfilled one great principle of Christian duty, by having considered and treated all mankind as their brethren; and by the joyful anticipation of extending to their relatives and friends the heartfelt consolation of finding their memories endeared to them, by the honour and respect with which their characters may be pourtrayed at that time, when the honour and respect of mankind can alone be duly appreciated.

APPENDIX J.

General Orders by the Commander in Chief, Head Quarters on board the Honourable Company's Ship Walthamstow.

Saugur Roads, 24th February, 1787.

THE Right Honourable Lord Lake having taken his

departure from Fort William for the purpose of returning to Europe, feels himself now called upon to perform
the last act of public duty in his situation of Commander in Chief in India, by recording his final testimony
of the character and conduct of the army of India, and of
all the officers and soldiers who have served under his
command.

In attempting the discharge of that duty, his Lordship
feels it difficult, either to do justice to them or to his own
feelings, under the mixed sensations of pride and regret,
inseparable from the occasion of contemplating their
merits, and of bidding adieu to officers and men, collectively and individually endeared to him by habits of intercourse and the mutual exertions of the spirit of professional enterprize, during the long period of six years, for
the most part passed amidst the vicissitudes of climate
and the laborious duties of the field, in the service of their
king and country.

The merits and the services of the army, and of all the
officers and troops engaged in the late arduous war in
India, have been so repeatedly and emphatically expressed, and recorded by the supreme government of the
British possessions in Asia, and the gratitude and applause
of the Commander in Chief have been so frequently called
forth to express his admiration of the gallant spirit of enterprize and exertions of the officers, the steady discipline
and undaunted valour of the troops, that the Commander
in Chief feels any endeavour of his, to add to their reputation, would only tend to lessen its estimation, in proportion as the attempt must fall short of the praise which
it deserves.

It therefore only remains for his Lordship to express
once more his most sincere and hearty thanks for the dis-

tinguished honour which he has derived from the gallant exertions and splendid successes of the British army in India; and to record that testimony, which personal observation and experience, during the period of six years, entitles him to pronounce: that the approbation which has been bestowed on them has been most eminently deserved, and that they have established a just and undoubted claim to the best rewards which can be conferred on them by a grateful government.

The Commander in Chief feels, that to ascribe any peculiar merit to the conduct by which the officers and soldiers, his countrymen, have been actuated, beyond what might attach to their distinguished valour and noble perseverance during a long and arduous war, would be felt only as a negative compliment. But he finds it difficult to do justice to the merits of our Native soldiers, who have encountered every danger with the most exemplary valour; who have submitted to every hardship and privation with the utmost fortitude and perseverance; and who, to promote the cause in which they were engaged, have on many occasions made a ready and cheerful sacrifice of every habit and prejudice which they had been taught to regard as dear and inviolable.

If any weight can attach to his success, or any influence be derived from the acknowledged national benefits that have been justly ascribed to the fortitude and valour of the British army in India, during the period of his command, the Commander in Chief will esteem it the greatest honour, and the highest gratification of his life, to employ that weight and influence in promoting the interests and exalting the character of that gallant army to which he now subscribes his affectionate farewell.

The remainder of his days will be enlivened by the recollection of those public services, which obtained for him the approbation of his king and country: and his Lordship will never cease to cherish the affectionate remembrance of the companions of his glory and the promoters of his success, during the eventful period of his long command in India.

(Signed)   HENRY WORSLEY,
Lt. Col. Adj. Gen. Bengal Army.

APPENDIX K.

THE 1st of November, 1808, the anniversary of the battle of Lasswarrie, having been appointed for the ceremony of presenting the honorary colours to the 1st and 2d Battalions of the 15th Regiment of Native infantry, then stationed at Barrackpoore, the regiment was drawn up at an early hour for the reception of Lord Minto, the Governor-general, who did the corps the honour to present the colours at the head of the grenadier companies previously advanced to receive them.

On presenting the colours to Lieutenant-Colonel Burrell, his Lordship delivered the following animated address, equally appropriate to the occasion, and honourable to the corps :—

COLONEL BURRELL,

" It is not unusual, on occasions like the present, to deliver a few thoughts adapted to the nature of the ceremony. In a common case, therefore, I might, perhaps, without impropriety, have prefaced this solemnity with observing, that the ensigns of a military body are not to be regarded as mere decorations to catch the notice of the vulgar, but that they have ever been esteemed, by good soldiers, the emblems and the pledges of those virtues and eminent endowments which form the best, and indeed the peculiar ornaments, of the military character. I might have said, that whoever casts his eyes on his colours, is reminded of loyalty to his sovereign and his country; fidelity to the government he serves; obedience to command; valour in the field; constancy under fatigue, privation and hardship. That he alone maintains the honour of his colours who lives and dies without reproach; and that when a soldier has pronounced the vow never to abandon them, but to fall in their defence, he has promised in other words, that under all circumstances, and in every extremity, he will prefer duty to life itself.

" Such topics, Sir, as these, might have suited other ceremonies of a similar nature. But I am sensible that I should depreciate the true character of the present proceeding, and I feel that I should degrade the high honours which I have the happiness to present to you, in the name of your country, if I thought it necessary to expatiate on the duties and virtues of military life, addressing myself as I now am, to men, who have afforded to their country and to the world, so many clear and signal proofs of every quality that can illustrate their honourable profession.

" These colours are delivered, therefore, to your care, not as pledges of future desert,—they are at once the reward of services already performed, and the memorial of glory already acquired.

"They display, indeed, the title and insignia of one great and splendid victory; in the celebration of which, we find ourselves, at this very hour, commemorating another triumph, in which also you were partakers. It might, indeed, have been difficult to select a day for this ceremony, which would not have recalled some one of the many distinguished actions, which have entitled you to share the fame of your renowned and lamented commander, and which would not have reminded us, that as his revered name is stamped indelibly on your banners, so you were, indeed, associated with him in all the dangers, exertions and successes of his glorious campaigns.*

" I beg you, Sir, to express to the 15th regiment, the cordial satisfaction I experience, in bearing with my own hand, this public testimony of the high regard and esteem I entertain for this distinguished body of men; and I request you to convey, above all, the assurances of my firm confidence, that colours obtained at Dehly, and presented on the anniversary of Lasswarrie, can only acquire new lustre in their hands."

Lieutenant-Colonel Burrell, in reply.

" MY LORD,

In the name of the 15th regiment of Bengal sepoys, I humbly entreat your Lordship to accept our unfeigned and respectful thanks for the high honour your Lordship has had the goodness to confer on us, by presenting these honorary colours; and for the favourable terms in which you have been pleased to mention our endeavours in the service of our country.

* The word Lake was embroidered in a wreath, under the other devices, on the honorary colours.

" These colours, my Lord, we receive with gratitude, and will preserve with honour, or fall in their defence."

APPENDIX L.

General Orders.

Head-Quarters, Isle of Mauritius, August 11th, 1811.

THE 2d Bengal Volunteer Battalion, under the command of Captain Lumley, being upon the eve of departure for India, His Excellency Major-General H. Warde cannot allow them to depart without expressing the very high sense he entertains of the particularly meritorious orderly, and soldier-like conduct which has been manifested by the whole of that corps, from the highest rank of officers to the private soldier, from the moment of landing upon the island, until the present period.

His Excellency Major-General Warde avails himself of this opportunity of assuring the whole of the Officers, Native Officers, and troops, which have already returned to India, and those that remain, that he entertains generally, similar sentiments of their uniform, meritorious, and soldier-like conduct, during the time he has had the honour of commanding them; and as he may probably never have the pleasure of serving with them again, after their departure from this island, he now with sincerity declares, that he shall ever feel a lively interest in their welfare and success.

APPENDIX M.

Extracts relating to the Native Troops of the Bengal Establishment, employed at the reduction of the Island of Java, under the command of Lieutenant-General Sir Samuel Auchmuty, and under the auspices of Lord Minto, Governor General, in the year 1811.

G. O.   By the Bengal Government.

It is highly satisfactory to the Vice-President in Council to observe, that the brave Sepoys who volunteered their services on the expedition to Java, have shared and emulated the glory of the European troops, and have thus afforded an additional and signal instance of that fidelity, zeal, and gallantry, for which the Honourable Company's Native troops have uniformly been distinguished.

From the Calcutta Gazette of October, 1811.

We have read with sincere pleasure the many concurring accounts that have been received, in commendation of the Bengal Sepoys serving with the expedition against Java; and we are happy to record, that in the several actions with the enemy, they distinguished themselves by their steadiness and gallantry: all accounts agree in stating, that their discipline, coolness, and intrepidity, were universally admired; and to be honourably distinguished in an army where every man proved himself a hero, is the highest praise that a soldier can receive.

A Sepoy Volunteer from the 1st Battalion 27th Regiment of Bengal Native Infantry, named Bahadur Khan, who was detached with the flankers, distinguished himself on the day of the action; he certainly bayoneted six of the Frenchmen, and did not fire a shot: some of the Europeans of His Majesty's 69th and 78th say, he killed nine. He was promoted to Naick, or Corporal, the next day.

APPENDIX N.

In the year 1809, two ferocious, or wild elephants made their appearance at the station of the Ramgurh Battalion at Hazaree Baugh. Those animals, which were of an uncommon size,* did much mischief, but were at length vanquished and put to death, after having made several furious charges on the two four-pounder field-pieces which were brought out against them: nineteen 4-lb. cannon balls, discharged from those pieces, were taken out of the bodies of the animals after they fell, and it was supposed eight or ten more were buried in their carcasses.

The commanding officer of the corps made an official report on the subject to the Commander in Chief, and after bestowing great praise on the artillery-men who served the guns, for their extraordinary steadiness and

---

* The dimensions of the largest were as follows:—Length from end of trunk to end of tail, 26 feet 9½ inches; height, 11 feet; round the body, 17 feet 8 inches; from crown of head to beneath the jaw, 7 feet.

bravery,—he related an instance of singular intrepidity on the part of a Sepoy of the Ramgurh Battalion, of which paragraph the following is a correct copy:—

In addition to my testimony of the good conduct of the artillery-men, I think it a duty to state, that one of the wild elephants having thrown down a Subadar (Native officer) of the corps, and his horse, and being on the point of destroying the former, a Sepoy, named Buldee Tewaree, stepped forward to his assistance, charged the animal with so much strength and resolution as to break his bayonet in his trunk, and 'turn his attention from the Subadar, whose life was thus providentially preserved.

N. B. This man was promoted for his manly and generous conduct.

APPENDIX O.

In the year 1798, the Governments of India, in imitation of the example of the mother country, called for voluntary contributions towards the support of the European war, and of His Majesty's Government; on which occasion, the Native troops in the service of the East India Company, emulating the example of their officers, had the honour of contributing towards the expenses of the war between England and France: of which the following testimony is recorded by the Bengal Government, over which Lord Mornington (since Marquis Wellesley) then presided.

GENERAL ORDERS,
By the Commander in Chief.

Fort William, 23d November, 1798.

THE Commander in Chief having received the orders of the Right Honourable the Governor General in Council, to express to the officers, non-commissioned officers, and private soldiers of the several European and Native corps serving under this Presidency, his cordial approbation on the occasion of their voluntary and patriotic contributions towards the support of His Majesty's government; can in no way so well fulfil the gratifying duty assigned to him, as by publishing the sentiments of his Lordship in Council, in General Orders, to the end, that the distinguished testimony which is borne to the zeal and public spirit of the European officers and soldiers, and to the fidelity and attachment of the Native troops to the service of the Company and the British Government, may be as public as it is merited and honourable.

He desires that particular pains may be taken to explain to the Native corps, the sentiments of approbation entertained by the Right Honourable the Governor-General, at the forwardness manifested by them to join their officers in so laudable a cause.

The Right Honourable the Governor-General in Council requests that the Commander in Chief will be pleased to express to the officers, non-commissioned officers, and privates of the several European and Native corps, his cordial approbation of the zeal and public spirit which they have manifested in voluntarily contributing a portion of their respective incomes, towards the support of his Majesty's government: and that it will afford to his

Lordship the greatest satisfaction, to communicate to the Honourable the Court of Directors, so honourable a testimony of the loyalty and liberal disposition of the European officers and soldiers, and of the fidelity and attachment of the Native troops to the service of the Company, and to the British Government.

NOTE.—It has been deemed proper to add this testimony, as the record of a fact which, however comparatively small the mite contributed by the Native soldiery, may be justly said to establish a claim to consideration, which should not be unknown to the British nation.

P.S.—*March*, 1817.—THE Writer, with the highest satisfaction and avidity, seizes the opportunity afforded him before this little work is finally committed to the press, to offer the tribute of his humble, though ardent and grateful respect, for the enlightened wisdom and liberal policy of the administration that now adorns the Government of Bengal ; which, under the auspices of the beneficent soldier and statesman, the Marquis of Hastings, has, in the course of the last year, enacted a regulation establishing a few easy, practicable rules for expediting the issue of all civil suits in which Native Officers and Sepoys may be concerned, in the several Courts of Justice throughout the Provinces under the Presidency of Fort William ; whereby a material cause of dissatisfaction in the minds of the Native soldiery, as alluded to in the preceding pages, has been modified or removed,

and their attachment to the service proportionately enhanced and secured : which, combined with many other
acts of minor, but very salutary attention, in regard to the
satisfaction and welfare of the troops composing the army
of Bengal, will doubtless cause the titles of HASTINGS
and MOIRA to be resounded with invocations of admiration and prosperity, from the mouths of the Ganges, to
the innermost parts of India.

CORRECTIONS AND ALTERATIONS.

P. 5, line 7 from the bottom, *for* subiadar's *read* subadar's.

— 101 and 153, *for* Mooshedabad *read* Moorshedabad.

— 116.   Sir D. Ochterlony has, since the Note was written, been created G. C. B.

— 169, line 5 from the bottom, *for* from *read* to.

— 205, line 6 from the top, *for* combinations *read* combination.

— 349, line 17, *instead of* Ensigns Carstairs and Muir were detached at the out-factories, *read* Ensign Muir was detached at one of the out-factories.

ADDENDUM.

Note upon the word " day," p. 282.

For which see " Notes on the Mahratta War," comprising Official Details and Documents published on the occasion by the government of Bengal; in which, describing the battle of Dehly, it is affirmed, that " The glory of " that day was not surpassed by any recorded triumph of " the British arms in India, and which was attended by " every circumstance calculated to elevate the fame of " British valour, to illustrate the character of British hu- " manity, and to secure the stability of the British empire " in the east."

London: Printed by C. Roworth, Bell-yard, Temple-bar.

CPSIA information can be obtained at www.ICGtesting.com
Printed in the USA
BVOW09s1033060415

394876BV00016B/136/P